Taking Risks
Defining Life

Taking Risks
Defining Life

A Soldier's Memoir

John McClarren

JMAC Publishing

johnrmcclarren.com

Taking Risks Defining Life – A Soldier's Memoir
© Copyright 2015 John McClarren
johnrmcclarren.com

All rights reserved. No part of this document or the related files may be reproduced or transmitted in any form, by any means (electronic, photocopying, recording, or otherwise) without the prior written permission of the author.

ISBN-13: 978-1511705127
ISBN-10: 1511705124

Book design and graphics by WhiteBoard Design Graphics.
Back cover photo by Deb McClarren.
Photos provided by John McClarren.

Additional copies of this book can be purchased from any bookstore or ordered directly from JMAC Publishing: johnrmcclarren.com.

Published by JMAC Publishing
johnrmcclarren.com

As with my first book, I wish to dedicate this book to all the men and women who have served faithfully in the armed forces of the United States of America; to all who have sacrificed some, and particularly to those who sacrificed all.

On a somewhat lighter note, I also dedicate this book to all who have mustered the intestinal fortitude to reach out and take the necessary risks in life to help themselves reach the goals they have set for their own lives and to help others they have found in need, even if it has involved risking their lives for those people.

Table of Contents

Introduction 11
Chapter 1 – Precarious Birth to Hazardous Childhood 15
Chapter 2 – Adventurous and Challenging Youth 47
Chapter 3 – Military Training 63
Chapter 4 – US Army, Vietnam 87
Chapter 5 – End of Active Duty 127
Chapter 6 – Formal Education to Teaching Career 145
Chapter 7 – Leave of Absence and Travel 155
Chapter 8 – Transition to Real Life 181
Chapter 9 – Family Trips, an Extended Adventure 215
Chapter 10 – The Big Move East 227
Chapter 11 – Michigan Employment and Opening Stores 245
Conclusion 279
About the Author 283
Abbreviations 285
Thank You 287
Preview of Military Life Service or Career – A Soldier's Perspective 289

Introduction

Let's face facts and look at the world in which we live, not through our proverbial "rose colored glasses," but through elements of reality, as scary as that might seem. We do live in a crazy world, would you not agree? Most of us also would probably have to agree that we ourselves have even contributed to a great deal of that craziness. If you have not, then you are undoubtedly in the minority. I look at my own life and I see some of the nutty things I have done throughout that life, and I cannot deny I have been a primary contributor to the apparent chaos of our world. I have a feeling most of you could say the same thing if you think about it. I'll show you some examples of some of the things I have done throughout my life that have seemed extreme to some, but most of those things have worked out quite well for me, which is not to imply in any way things could not have turned out much worse. It could well have been luck playing a part or even divine intervention. You can be the judge.

When I had barely reached double digits in age, I went charging out into the Pacific Ocean, hardly knowing how to swim, unaccompanied by anyone, let alone an adult, venturing out just as deep as I could go, barely able to touch the bottom with my feet, in order to catch the best possible wave for body surfing. Did I think about any possible consequences of such a thing? Oh, hell no. Why would I ever do that? Maybe ten years later, shortly after achieving adulthood, and upon watching the developments in Vietnam escalate into a war, I left college to join the US Army, and even volunteered to go into the infantry to become a line officer, knowing of course, I would be going to Vietnam. People were already dying over there. Did most people around me consider what I had done to be the wisest thing for me at the time? I would have to say, probably not, but it did seem to be for me the best direction at that moment in time. On one occasion, during my tour in Vietnam, I put a gun to someone's head, someone whom I did not know to be the enemy, without really thinking through all the possible consequences of such an act. It was spontaneous at the time it happened, and just seemed like the right thing to do, and I have always strongly believed it was. Those are merely three of the many occasions for which I was guilty of taking a risk to accomplish something important, and, more often than not, those risks paid off. After seventy years of that sort of thing, I don't think I am anywhere near through. I still have a good deal of life to live.

As I sit here on this sunny, southern California beach, absorbing all of those warm rays from directly overhead and the cool breeze off the Pacific, watching the surfers cut the curls of those beautiful offshore breakers, an occasional dolphin or sea lion cutting across the surface of the water... All right, all right, I'm lying.

Actually, I am here in northern Michigan in early December, looking through my sliding glass door across my back yard, covered in a nice, thick blanket of brilliant white snow, and the temperature at a brisk twenty degrees without the wind chill factor. That may create a beautiful picture in some of your minds or even in a photograph, but it is not a very pretty picture to me right now. It's cold, man! It would not be so bad if I were out downhill or cross-country skiing, but I was just out in that nasty weather, going to the grocery store, and not having much fun. However, looking across the snow, I can still reflect back on those days on the Pacific coast beaches.

I was born and raised in San Diego, California, home to a very large contingency of the US Navy and US Marine Corps. Although I have few vivid memories of family military ties, there is little doubt I was influenced to some degree by my surroundings. I had one uncle who had been a sailor in World War II, and I had seen pictures of him in uniform. I had a second uncle by marriage, who was a career naval photographer, and I saw him frequently in uniform. That was the full extent of family military influence in my younger life. So, what was it that might have been responsible for my having spent over thirty years in the active and reserve components of the US Army? It had to have been much more than just one or two individuals or a single incident that influenced me to such a degree.

If I were to classify my life with a single, brief idea, it would be a continuing challenge to find enrichment and fulfillment through success in all endeavors I have ever undertaken, which would also include my own self-satisfaction, and few, if any, of those endeavors were without risk. That pattern seems to have remained reasonably consistent from birth to the present, my age now being the big seven-zero.

I would also not want to imply that I have now fulfilled all of my dreams, even though my life so far has been one of great satisfaction. I am not even close to being finished. I have reestablished an entirely new set of goals for life, because, the way I figure it, I still have at least forty years left before I will be ready to hang it up. My plan is to live to at least 110 years old. After all, I still have a good deal to accomplish on the old "bucket list." I have also considered extending that age to 111, just so my wife and I can celebrate our 75th wedding anniversary. That fact, of course, scares the hell out of Deb, my wife. It will be a completely new world by the time I am ready to call it quits, right? Who knows what may be on the horizon? I always remain flexible.

In order to attain the goals I have always set, there has been an underlying prerequisite as I briefly mentioned above, the element of taking risks. There are times when those risks will come back and bite you, but ultimately, the plan will undoubtedly all come together. I always loved how George Peppard of "The A-Team" used to say it: "I love it when a plan comes together."

CHAPTER 1 – PRECARIOUS BIRTH TO HAZARDOUS CHILDHOOD

I am sure there must be some intellectual schmuck out in the world somewhere who has at some point in the past made a statement, and probably even had it published, that went something like, "The greatest thing that has ever happened to me is my birth." It may well be true that without birth there is no life, but let me also relate from personal experience that birth is not always a pretty picture. After nearly ten months of development in my mother's womb, I was ready for birth, and I am absolutely sure my mother was, but there seemed to be some obstacles holding up the process.

I was held back (the term later used when I failed to make it through my second grade class – yes, recycled at that tender, young age), and with the help of my mother's wonderful doctor, we nearly killed her. The poor woman was in hard labor for ten straight days, after nine and a half very long months into her pregnancy. She was all of four feet, eleven inches tall, and she gave birth to a nearly ten-pound baby boy (yours truly) who practically ripped her to shreds, leaving her with the scars of a hundred stitches it took to put her back together. Yes, I still do feel just a trifle guilty for that. Sorry, mom.

How is that for painting a vivid picture of the beauty of birth? Yes, the doctor probably should have been sued or arrested for the wonderful job he did with my mother. It's no wonder medical malpractice insurance is so high today. Coming into the world was definitely my first major challenge of life, and yet I consider it a success and certainly a blessing, not necessarily for my mother. It reminds me of the pilot who claims any landing you can walk away from is a good landing. Any birth that mother and child can both live through is a good birth, not easy or enjoyable, just good.

To create a complete list of obstacles to my life could take up several volumes, and I would never test your patience with that, but a sampling might well be in order to give a reasonably complete picture of what life can be, and yet I have no valid complaints about how life has been for me. Many of you reading this book have had it much worse than I have. Forget about any pity trip I alluded to earlier. Life has been great, and each of these obstacles has proven to be an effective increment to the total development of who I am today.

If any of the obstacles I have encountered were to have been taken away, my life would have changed, and not necessarily for the better. I am thankful for all of them. I am more than happy with myself and certainly with how my whole family has turned out. I also take little or no credit for any of it. It would seem a legion of angels has watched over my family. Without such a divine legion, we would not have stood a chance.

Considering how I have classified my life, one might get the impression I feel most successes in life do not come without a challenge. I do think that is often the case, but not always. If success were easy, then there would never be any great feelings of accomplishment. Therefore, it would appear I have made some great accomplishments in my life. Wow. How's that for logic?

To clarify things just a bit, as most of you, I have been through some significant struggles that have turned into what I would consider great successes. Some might consider these struggles as failures or near failures, but I do not see them quite that way. Some were misses or near misses, maybe failures, yet necessary in order to meet the designated goals for which I had striven. Rather than considering any of them complete failures, I look at them as temporary setbacks, lessons learned and mind-broadening experiences. Ah, yes, the old optimistic point of view. It never fails.

From my rather tough birthing process, I went through a series of incidents that should have been wake-up calls or alerts to look out for serious, life-threatening situations coming my way. One of my first relatively serious and memorable incidents was when, at about three years old, I decided to take a challenging tricycle run, something of a risk, down the side of my grandparents' house in Los Angeles, California. 2262 Lake View Avenue rolls off the tongue like it came from a book of poetry. For that reason alone, I will never forget that house or that address, or the particular incident that now follows.

The house was high on a hill, and there was a walkway along the side of the house that had close to a forty-degree slope, or seemingly so. There were bushes on the left side of the walkway and hollowed out, artificial cement logs filled with rocks on the right. I am sure my idea was that those rocks would cushion my fall should I have any trouble along the way. My tricycle was not a brand new, shiny one, but rather a nasty little thing with a broken front wheel that wobbled a good deal, even when riding it on level ground and in a normal manner. This was not to be a normal ride. It was more of an Evel Knievel trip with little chance of survival, and yet my three-year-old mind could see the glory and excitement of the experience. Nothing could go wrong; I was sure of that. Why else would I have considered it? I mean, I was a very intelligent three-year-old.

Everything seemed to be in order. There was no escape route along the way, or at the end of the ramp for that fact, as there was also a cement log full of rocks at the end. I feel you are formulating a picture in your mind at this moment. There was no chance of survival, but that did not seem to be a major problem. Away I went, first with a gentle breeze blowing in my face, followed by the skin on my face rolling back from the g-forces (all right, a slight exaggeration). My speed continued to increase as the front wheel of the tricycle began to wobble. That wheel-wobble developed into an entire body-tremble for the kid, and then the trike was completely out of control and my body sailed through the air, face-first toward a pile of rocks.

Fortunately, however, some suspended wires over the rocks caught my attention, as well as my nose, snapping it as I continued my flight, perhaps slowing my speed a wee bit, just before landing in the rocks. I was not at my best at that moment. The only thing I recall after that is the bloody water in the bathroom sink. It could have been the Nile River turned red by the staff of Moses for all I knew. It was definitely bright red; I do remember that part very well.

Although my visit to the doctor is a bit foggy, the family has told me I let out a blood-curdling scream heard throughout the building as he set my nose. Yes, it was, in fact, broken. Well, that little incident did leave a mark, perhaps more emotionally than physically, and I was probably not the cutest kid on the block for a few weeks. I was always a quick healer, however.

The next incident had to do with my older, late sister, Lois, on whom I have to lay the blame. She would agree if she were still with us. She was about five and a half years older than I, and became almost a second mother to me. She was quite the acrobat and very energetic. It could not have been more than a few months after the tricycle incident when she was doing cartwheels behind the couch in my grandparents' living room. She was without a doubt trying to impress me, and I was sitting there taking it all in. During this little exhibition, she kicked over a tall alabaster lamp. Where was I at the time? You guessed it; right in the line of fall of the lamp. She never yelled, "Timber!" It caught me by surprise, right above the right eye. That one also left a mark; about six stitches to be exact. I don't recall, but can only imagine the bloodstains on the carpet after that little accident.

Next, when I was about five years old, I was entertaining a young lady in my house, which was not unusual. I was very attracted to the little girls at the time and I was a notorious show-off for them. I am not certain things have changed remarkably since then. However, I was in the process of jumping up and down on the couch when I took one tremendous leap to impress womankind, but I was off a little in targeting my landing zone. I drifted a bit to the left and landed directly in the middle of a round, glass-top coffee table. The glass did not hold, and I went straight through to the floor. Broken glass covered my body, but I was miraculously unhurt. I did not have a scratch anywhere. Wow! Was that little girl impressed or what? And, yes, "Jesus loves the little children." That was just one of my early proofs.

A couple of years later, I escaped another potentially serious problem, which, I suppose, could have resulted in the loss of sight in one eye. We had the cutest little black cocker spaniel I remember very well. One of the most remarkable things I recall is how he dunked his ears into his water dish every time he went for a drink. Being only five or six years old, I was fascinated with watching everything he did, including his eating habits. I was watching him eat his dinner one evening and I was a little too close to him. With no warning, he flipped around and caught me right in the lower inside corner of my eye with his canines. It did not actually cut my eyeball, but came so close it that it is a little scary thinking about the potential results. I shed a little blood again, but was perfectly all right. He was a dog whose bite was worse than his bark; I also recall that bark being just plain irritating.

During the same timeframe, I had some very enjoyable experiences that tended to balance out some of those seemingly negative elements. My family was never wealthy by any means, but some of our activities might have seemed so. My first stepfather, Dick, enjoyed spearfishing off the coast of Los Angeles, and that included trapping and collecting lobsters. Now and then, he would come home from one of his trips with a ton of lobster, and we would have a lobster feast. It was very cool, and yet a little sad dropping each of those creatures into boiling water and watching them jump. Anyone who does that tries to justify it by claiming the lobster's nervous system does not allow it to feel the boiling water. However, watching them react does make me wonder about those claims. It always seemed to me like a hell of a way to go. On the other hand, did we ever enjoy those wonderful meals! You have to take the bitter with the sweet, I suppose. It was the lobster's loss, but our gain. It was great.

If there were anything specific that profoundly influenced my actions throughout life, it would be the term that is the name of today's clothing line, "No Fear." It was also an unfortunate attitude, which probably should have gotten me killed several times over, or at least seriously injured more often than it did. Many times, when I should have been using much more caution, I would jump into a situation, not terribly concerned about the dangers, and end up paying the price.

One such occasion was in elementary school. On my way home at the end of the day, I was passing by the schoolyard when I spotted a kid who was apparently trying to get my attention. He had a stick in his hand that looked like a cut-off broom handle or a baton of some sort. He was threatening to throw it at me. A chain-link fence, typical for most schoolyards, separated us and protected me quite well. How could that kid have been any threat to me whatsoever? I just defiantly said, "Go ahead, idiot; throw it at me!"

Although it may not have been the wisest response on my part, it did turn out to be a valuable learning experience for me. Wow! What an arm that guy had! It seemed like one of those hundred-mile-an-hour pitches you only hear about, but never see, and it did exactly what the kid intended, but what I never expected. As though it were mathematically calculated, the stick sailed with perfect precision straight through one of the very small spaces in the fence and caught me right above the right eye. Well, that was humbling, and I had the biggest "goose egg" you could imagine for a good couple of weeks.

From nine or ten years old, I consider myself to have been for the most part a "latchkey kid." Independence was probably my best friend at that age. I cooked, cleaned and took care of the house and myself the best I could. My mother worked nights just for us to survive. My sister was usually out on a date or busy doing teenage girl "stuff" and that was not always good. Even though I was frequently out late at night with one of my friends, I was able somehow to avoid serious trouble. Oh, we always managed to find some trouble, but seldom were we caught. One of the things my friend and I used to do was hitchhike to the beach, especially when we could not afford to go by bus. It was also a very long bike ride, but now and then, we did that also.

One day we were thumbing it to the beach, and a single, older man, who looked a little grubby, picked us up. It did not worry us all that much; it was a ride. Well, as we progressed, the man looked over at us a little strangely a few times, which made us a little uncomfortable. After a moment or two, he began digging into a big envelope, and said, "Hey, I want to show you boys some pictures of my wife." We were very typical of what those in the military would call delta, alpha kilos (dumb-ass-kids), and just said, "Okay."

Well, the pictures of "his wife" were eye-openers indeed for ten-year-olds! Not only were they naked photos, but hard-core pornography, especially back in the 50's! We did receive a memorable education, and one, which I would in no way recommend for children. There are many very good reasons not to allow children in vehicles with strangers. We were very fortunate. It could have been much worse. Times were very different back then than today, but that was taking very serious chances, and it did make an impression on us. As I recall, that was the last time we hitchhiked to the beach. I have to admit it did frighten us a little, just because we were not sure what to expect from this guy, and I really don't recall sharing that information with my mother. That risk was another success, but only because there could have been a heavy price to pay, and that did not happen.

A single mom raised me. Well, all right, she was married off and on. I used to call my mother and sister the Gabor sisters, just because they had both gone through so many husbands before finding the right one. Anyway, one of her boyfriends, Floyd, seemed to like me a lot or just wanted to impress my mother, but one day he decided to take me out spearfishing off the cliffs of one of the beaches of southern California. It may have been around Palos Verdes, south of Los Angeles. It was one of those new, exciting and potentially dangerous experiences. We had a very enjoyable day. I saw things I had never seen before, including all of the beautiful fish, corals, moray eels, sea anemones, lobsters and great kelp beds. The surf was rough that day with very large breakers coming into shore.

When we had experienced enough snorkeling, caught enough fish, and were ready to call it a day, we began to move toward shore. This was not just a typical sandy beach. In order to get to the beach, we had to maneuver through large rock outcroppings covered by very sharp barnacles. With our feet digging into the sandy bottom, we had to brace ourselves against rocks as those powerful waves crashed over us. Then we would move forward a little more and brace ourselves for the next wave or set of waves, and so it went as we made our way into the beach.

Watching over the kid (me), Floyd called out over the roar of the surf, "Brace yourself, John. Here comes another one." That wave broke him loose from his rock, sending him right into me, which, of course, broke my grip, and I went with the wave right over those barnacle-covered rocks. This time I began turning the Pacific Ocean to blood, again alluding to Moses and the Nile, but it was physically a little tougher on me than on Moses. Wow, did that one leave marks! I never went to the hospital or even to a doctor, but those scars lasted about thirty years, as the barnacles took skin off down to the bone on my legs and feet. There could have been a minor lesson there in whom to trust. He was not the greatest father figure in the world, nor, to my knowledge, did he ever make it to that status. He was a nice man though.

A good part of my early childhood, I spent in south Los Angeles. One of my most enjoyable activities, particularly during the summer, was, as mentioned earlier, going to the beach. My friend, Corky, and I took the bus to the beach one day, as opposed to hitchhiking. Those were really the good old days, when we were able to make those kinds of choices on our own without consulting our parents. We were big shots back then, and it had to have been one of those "no fear" things going on with both of us. We decided to go to Manhattan Beach.

We were very good friends, but Corky and I did have some different ideas of what we considered fun. He very often just wanted to go play with the girls, and, as much as I too liked the girls, I was at the beach primarily to body surf. That was my favorite beach activity by far. I was very good at it and would have been even better had I only known how to swim! Oh, I know. Don't go there with me. How can you body surf without knowing how to swim? I don't know. I just did it and did it well, well, most of the time.

On that particular day, my friend and I managed to separate from one another. He must have been off playing with the girls somewhere, and I went into the water to catch some good waves. Surf was up, and unfortunately so were the rip tides. I knew them well and how to avoid them, at least in principle. If I recall correctly, I think I did catch a couple of very good waves that day. However, on my last trip out to the good waves I went just a trifle too far for a weak swimmer. It was normal for this little daredevil to go out neck-deep to catch the waves. That is where I was on that day, and, while I was waiting for a good one to come by, I began to feel a very strong tug on my body. The current was actually dragging me off my feet and pulling me out so far I could no longer touch bottom.

Before I knew it, I was well over my head. I tried repeatedly to pull myself back toward shore, but it was not happening. All I could do was drop down to the bottom until my feet could touch the sand and spring my body up to the surface to grab a quick breath of air. That seemed to work for a while, but it could not last forever. After four or five repetitions, I could feel myself weakening, and I knew it would not be long before it was all over.

Right when I was certain I was coming up for my last breath, a hand came out of nowhere and grabbed my arm. I knew it was a man, but I was not sure whether he was very tall and walking or if he was swimming, but somehow I was moving toward the beach. As soon as I could touch bottom with my feet and had control, he released me, and I never saw him again. I have no idea today who he was or even what he looked like. He was there for the good deed, and he was gone!

I struggled back to shore with the remaining energy I had, and collapsed on the beach. I lay there for about five minutes, thinking I could hear Twilight Zone music in the background, and that was before there was such a program as Twilight Zone. It does confirm for me there really have been angels looking after me all my life. I'm still not convinced that just one would have been sufficient. For the life of me, I cannot figure out why God did not just say, "Hey, I think I'll just let him die. He's more trouble to us down there than he will be up here and out of harm's way." However, I am still alive and reasonably well. He must have had some other purpose for me. That, however, remains unclear at this point.

Those early years were also years of discovery. As you have already seen, I had made some significant discoveries. Another of those was coming to terms with death. Many people, and probably most parents, have the attitude that children should be protected from being exposed to death and dying. Although that may sound like a very good idea, maybe it's not. It is in no way a pleasant subject, but it is a reality of life, and the logical question arises as to whether or not we should protect our children from the realities of life. Those realities to which I refer are those every human being will ultimately encounter at one time, or another, and death would be in that category. Early exposures to death could perhaps preclude extreme trauma for some later in life. Those are the things, however, that most of us would rather not think about until the time comes.

I had my first encounter with death when I was about ten years old. My friend and I were biking out to the beach one day when we came upon a serious car accident, involving three or four vehicles. There were police and emergency vehicles already at the scene. We rode our bikes up to one of the badly damaged cars. As we looked inside, what we saw was a greater shock than children should ever encounter. The man in the driver's seat was dead, as the windshield had gone straight through his neck. It was not a pretty sight. We had made another discovery. We knew at that point what death looked like. It was indeed a growing experience, as well as a memory that would last a lifetime. It did not completely traumatize us, but it did introduce us to a reality that could hit any of us at any time.

The next encounter with death was not long after the first one, and it occurred on a fishing trip out to Catalina Island off the coast of Long Beach, California. One of the men on board had not felt well most of the trip, and decided to go below just to sit down and relax and perhaps recover. The next time I saw him was when I went below to use the bathroom. I saw him slumped over the table, lying face down in his own vomit, and dead. He apparently had had a heart attack. That again was a sobering sight for a ten- or eleven-year-old, but that was also not quite the end of that encounter.

The next thing we had to do was figure out what to do with our dead passenger. It put something of a damper on the fishing trip. We headed for shore, contacting the authorities by radio, and they told us to go, I believe, to the Manhattan Beach pier. A couple of the men secured our dead friend to a stretcher and hoisted him about fifty feet to the top of the pier. That, too, was a sight to remember, watching the stretcher dangle and swing back and forth precariously, as the hoist lifted it to the top of the pier. We all wondered if his body would just slip out and into the ocean as all of this was unfolding. I was casehardened to death very early in life. Honestly, it was, I think, good preparation for what was to come later on. Just a year or two later my grandfather died of natural causes at the early age of fifty-six. I was able to deal with it very well, even with an open casket at his funeral.

Before I reached ten years old, my mother had been in and out of marriages and other romantic relationships more times than I could count. Then again, I was never great at math. She was never married to a military man, but she had a few military boyfriends in between marriages. My sister was coming of age much quicker than her years, and she too was dating the sailors in their cute little white uniforms (Yuk! Try not to take that personally if you were in the Navy.) If memory serves me well, it seems like a few "jarheads" (marines) showed up occasionally. No wonder I later decided on the Army! Those "swabbies" were everywhere, and, when you throw in a few marines, that was way too much for little brother and young son. Even walking around downtown San Diego with my friends, we could not go anywhere without being surrounded by sailors and marines. It was really overkill, but we all became used to it, and it was hardly noticeable after a while.

It was also about the same timeframe that my older cousin, Patty, had entered college, and had a boyfriend who was going through the Air Force R.O.T.C. program at San Diego State College (now University). I was impressed with the guy, and I really admired what he was doing. He graduated, received a commission as a second lieutenant in the Air Force, went to flight school and began flying the B-52 Stratofortress strategic bomber. Oh, later on I discovered he was a real jerk, but at the time, I thought what he was doing and what he had become the greatest thing ever. From that point on, and I could not have been much over ten years old, I wanted the Air Force to be my career goal, and I wanted to fly. That was it, and there would be no changing my mind. I established that as my one major goal in life.

It was shortly after my grandfather's death that my mother, sister and I moved from the Los Angeles area to San Diego. We began a new life and were very happy there. That happiness lasted until we left town one weekend, and returned to find the little house we had lived in, which belonged to my grandmother, had burned nearly to the ground. The fire gutted the house and destroyed or damaged nearly everything in it. Honestly, it was not a great loss, in that we really did not have all that much to lose. We were, however, quite short on clothing for a while. That sort of a loss can be very traumatic, however. You lose things money cannot buy, not that we had a great deal of money with which to replace things. It is much tougher on adults than it is on children, and, therefore, my mother took the brunt of it.

Many of the things that happened in our lives seemed horrible at the time and appeared to be nearly insurmountable challenges and obstacles, but actually were experiences that helped to build character in all of us. Many of them developed strength and taught us how to deal with the odds that always seemed to be stacked against us. For all of the bad things that happened throughout our lives, there were always good things that resulted from those events. After our little house burned down, I was the one who eventually occupied it long after it had been rebuilt, and at a time when I really needed the privacy as a young man in college. I needed the quiet and seclusion, and that was my haven, a place in which to bury myself in my studies and concentrate on working on my advanced education. At the same time, my mother, sister and grandmother lived in the big house on the property. I was to a large degree on my own at that time.

Before I charge into that phase of my life, however, I'll concentrate on the time just after my family made our move to San Diego and some of the challenging and memorable obstacles I met along the way. I was a good kid, as I think I have implied a few times already, and seldom found serious trouble, but that is not to say I was not perfectly capable of finding trouble if it were nearby and waiting for someone like me to find it.

I used to love ice cream and that has not changed "a lick" since I was a wee child. We could not always afford to stop the Good Humor ice cream truck every time it came by, which was every day. It would always drive by the house in the afternoon, playing the favorite, familiar songs over its loudspeaker as it drove by. On the days I could not afford to buy an ice cream, my favorite little risky trick was to run up behind the truck and hop up onto the over-sized rear bumper, parking my posterior in place, for a nice ride down the street. The driver, from what I could tell, never knew about it.

One day the ice cream truck was cruising down the street, and I positioned myself, ready to make my move, and thinking once again that the driver did not see me. I was hiding in front of a parked car. How could he have seen me? The truck usually drove very slowly, not to pass up any potential sales. As he passed, I charged out from my well-concealed ambush site and ran up behind the truck, ready to take another giant leap for boyhood. I made a great jump and was moving at the right speed and in the right place when the driver abruptly hit the brakes. Wham! I slammed into the back of the truck like a cold slab of beef. I was stunned, though conscious, and to my recollection the driver resumed his route without checking on me or even looking back. I could be wrong, but I think he continued right along, smiling and with the satisfaction of knowing I was one kid who would probably never attempt that stunt again. We both gained by that experience: he taught a kid a lesson; I learned a good lesson. I was greatly humbled. Ooh, did that smart!

Another memorable incident left a few minor scars. I was always a kid with a mission, and there was frequently little time to get it all done. Consequently, I was usually in a rush to get from point A to point B. Sometimes I think I had lost the concept of walking. Running was the norm. Things are probably not terribly different today. One day I was in a rush to get to that point B, and, I happened to be running out of the house to get there. We had a nice big front porch with a few steps leading down to the driveway. The front of the porch had a wall about three feet tall, over which hung rose bush vines. Well, rather than running out to the driveway, which would have been the normal and wisest thing to do, I chose to climb onto the wall and jump off, down to the front lawn. If there were ever a risk involved, that would be the route I would take.

In the process of making that long leap, which seemed to be a sensible and logical plan, I jumped straight through the rose bush catching a face full of thorns. I landed face down in the grass. My mother had watched the whole thing and ran out yelling, "Honey, are you all right?" My hands were covering my face as I answered, "Sure, mom, it doesn't hurt a bit," blood trickling through my fingers. It only took her an hour or so to pull all the thorns out of my face. Fortunately, none went into my eyes, although very close to it. My short cut took me a little longer that day. That one could not possibly have been my fault either. It was the booby trap.

The next couple of incidents involved my sister, Lois, again. In the first one, there were no injuries, but there probably should have been. I think I was barely twelve years old when Lois had the bright idea that her little brother should learn how to drive. I was always short for my age; so, my feet could hardly reach the pedals. Having taken the wheel, I started down the straight road of a residential neighborhood, and for a good distance, I did just fine. Then I came to a stop sign. I brought the car to a nice stop, and looked both directions and ahead for what was to come. The street did not exactly continue straight. It took a dogleg to the right, so that I had to turn right and then immediately left. I did not like the looks of it and told Lois to take the wheel; I did not want to attempt it. She, of course, did not want to hear that kind of response.

"You will do just fine. Just turn the wheel right, ease it around and go left the same way."

"No," was my reply, "I really don't want to do this."

"Just do it!" she barked back.

Off I went, making my right turn. It did not feel right at all, and I attempted to brake. Unfortunately, I did not hit the brake; instead, I hit the accelerator and began my left turn at the same time. We careened around the corner at lightning speed, smashing into a parked car and molding it around a tree! That was probably the worst turn I would ever make in my driving career. Neither of us was hurt, and we immediately switched places, as it would go much better for us if she were to have been driving, rather than a twelve-year-old kid. (Duh!) The parked car I hit was totaled, and the car we were driving was in very serious condition. Neither of us having been hurt was the best news, as well as surprising. The car belonged to her boyfriend, and I am not sure what happened there. That was not the point, nor any of my business. Both of us having escaped injury made it a complete, or near, success.

The next incident, also involving Lois, was when she and I were going somewhere in a convertible with the top down. I believe it was once again another one of her boyfriends' cars. We had parked at a business just off the road in a small dirt parking lot. It was time to leave, and she backed up to position the car for an exit. In so doing, she did not notice a telephone pole guy-wire, secured to the ground, right behind us. She managed to drive right under it, and, consequently, the wire with its metal cover scraped across the back of the car and along the passenger side, and over the top of my right arm that was resting on and extended through the window. Ouch! That was another one that left scars, from my wrist to my elbow, still visible today. Was that a win or a loss? Oh, hell, it toughened me up further. Thank you again, Lois. I still cannot figure out why I loved my sister so much, but I sure did. So, she was a little accident-prone.

On a less traumatic note, I mentioned I was capable of finding trouble, although it was seldom serious. It is possible that finding trouble could have been partially due to my preponderance to take risks. I spent a good deal of my young life at the San Diego Zoo, as that was a favorite past time among many of my friends. Hey, as cool as the zoo can be, anything can lose its appeal after so much of seeing the same old things. We eventually got to the point of thinking (a very dangerous thing for young boys) we needed a little more adventure. We would tend to wander off the main route, which all visitors must stay on. There were many areas forbidden to anyone other than zoo employees. Those areas were where real adventure was. After all, they were forbidden zones, right? Where else would young boys want to be, other than off-limits areas?

More than once, we left the zoo with an escort. For kids, at that time, there was no admission charge; so, there was no loss when they kicked us out. It did not cost us a dime. There was one particular occasion where we were wandering around and spotted a large, beautiful, blue emu egg, just lying there within reach! The temptation was just too much. It might as well have had a sign on it that said, "Take me." I had to reach inside the fence just a few inches to retrieve the egg. It was easy, and I had it in my possession. So, what was I going to do with it? Who knew? However, I had it, and the big challenge was to get it out of the zoo without someone detecting what we had done.

My friend and I, looking very sheepish, made our way to the front gate, concealing the egg the best we could. I was the one who absconded with the contraband; so, I had to carry it. We were both scared to death, and how we managed to get out with that huge blue egg I'll never know, but we did. When I got it home, I did not know what to do with it. I felt so guilty it was killing me. I don't recall how, but my mother did find out, and I was in a heap of trouble. I think I have blanked out of my mind what we finally did with the egg, but I think we just threw it away. My mother could kill me emotionally with never laying a hand on me. I would have felt better if she had just smacked me when I did something stupid. She had a way of making me feel terrible with little more than "the look." She had that "mother" look that penetrated to the depths of my soul. She was good. Did I feel like a failure? Oh yeah, of course, I did because I failed to meet her expectations. However, it did once again work on my character, which still needed a good deal of additional attention.

We can all think back to the days of our first romantic love relationships and those initial encounters with the opposite sex. We lost our sense of balance and our sense of values, if we even had them at that point. Let's face it; we had little sense at all back then anyway. The junior high school years, today's middle school years, had to have been the most awkward times of our lives. We were pimply, greasy, we boys had no hair where we wanted hair and the girls sometimes had hair where they did not want hair. We were unbelievably clumsy. We were all extremely nervous around those of the opposite sex, and never knew how to act when in their presence. Things are much different today than they were in the fifties and sixties.

Then there were dances where the boys sat at one end of the hall and the girls sat at the other end. The only way the two sexes would mingle would be if the boy were to muster up enough fortitude to make that eternal walk across the room to invite a girl to dance. I think by now I have firmly established that the most important thing a guy had to consider was being cool! There was no alternative or choice in the matter. He would make his slow cruise across the floor, not looking at the girl of his desires, and certainly not showing any of that desire or anxiety along the way. That would never do.

When a young man reached his destination, he would stop, slowly look down at the girl, and say with an ever-so-slight smile, "Would you like to dance?" If she said "Yes" then the phenomenal task was to maintain your cool, when inside you were bursting apart with happiness and excitement. Why? Because the alternative was for her to say "No" or, if she were polite, "No, thank you." Then you would feel like the biggest fool at the dance even to think that she would have said "Yes" and you would have plenty of time to ponder it on your way back to that section where the other "losers" hung out. Oh, believe me; I was there many times over. I was a very slow learner, but very determined and persistent, never to neglect or lose the characteristic of cool.

Now and then at those junior high school dances, there was a "lady's choice," which was when the girls would take the trip across the room, and make their choice of what boy they wanted. For the boys, this had to have been more agonizing than the normal way. After all, nine times out of ten, it was not the girl with whom you wanted to dance, who was making her way toward you. Here she comes, and it is probably the homeliest girl at this event who wants to dance with you. Are you going to be ugly and turn her down, which you know will absolutely crush her? You already know how bad it feels for someone to turn you down. So, you just "bite the bullet" when she approaches and you dance! As much as we do want to be cool, we never really want to be cruel.

Yes, there were always those who were cruel, and would send the girls away in tears, and laugh it off. I could never justify that, as tough as it was to go through with it. Neither choice would work well, but a choice was nevertheless necessary. The same is true for the girls. This just happens to be a guy's perspective. Life always seemed to be cruel at that age. We all got through it, and the tough parts and bad decisions were all just part of the game. We hated it, but still had to play.

Quite possibly the best part of those times was the music. I have never stopped loving the music of the fifties and sixties. I even continued to love the songs for which the girls turned me down for a dance. Occasionally they did not turn me down, and, of course, those I loved even more. You readers who are near my age will always remember Elvis Presley in his early years, Fats Domino, Richie Valens, The Big Bopper, The Coasters, The Everly Brothers, Chuck Berry, Jerry Lee Lewis, Johnny Otis ("Willy and the Hand Jive") and I could go on forever. It was great music to dance to or just kick back on the southern California beaches, groovin' to the tunes. I just thought I would throw those little tidbits at you, as it was so important to the times, as well as to me.

But, wait. Why would I want to leave the 50s trivia without mentioning some of our favorite television programs? I do recall that the first television my family ever had was about 1948. The first programs I recall were puppet shows, including Kukla, Fran and Ollie, Beanie (and Cecil the Sea-Sick Sea Serpent), and Howdy Doody, and then, of course, we can never forget Milton Berle, Ed Sullivan and Arthur Godfrey. Just a little later, we added "I Love Lucy," "Captain Kangaroo," Jack Paar's "Tonight Show," "Gun Smoke" and "Bonanza." Ah, those were the days, my friend.

I do have another example of the epitome of teenage clumsiness. It must have been somewhere back in junior high school when I had a birthday party or something of that nature going on, and I really wanted to invite my ever-so-hot flame to come to my party. I invited her and she did come. I was nervous just having her over to my house. That did not happen often. As usual, at thirteen or fourteen years old, I had to be cool. That was again an absolute necessity.

After I had filled my plate with food, and come to the couch sectional to sit down, I had not considered that the end of the sectional protruded a little further to the left and did not have a back. I was ready to sit down next to my lady. Without looking back, I sat down, leaned back, and, much to my surprise, there was no back against which to lean. I went all the way, my plate of food soaring toward the ceiling, and my body doing a back-flip over the end of the couch, rolling backwards through the door into the next room, with my food landing everywhere, including all over my date. Everyone just froze and stared. I was, of course, stunned and rather devastated by the whole thing. Then the atmosphere lightened up a bit as we all began to laugh almost hysterically. Hey, did I impress my true love on that occasion? You bet I did! That may be part of why that relationship never quite developed the way I had once hoped it might.

Along with this discussion of "cool," why don't we tie it in with an example that fits the description? Once again, let's return to our junior high school days. Schools can be the perfect example of cliques that form in any society or institution. It does not matter if those cliques consist of age groups, racial groups, political groups, ideological groups, athletic groups or just plain social groups. We could go on with that one, but you see the point. Well, I did have a significant group of friends in those early days, and we probably did stand out a bit from the rest of the crowd. Whether that was in a good way or bad way remains to be seen.

Someone recently reminded me of an episode of my life which I had conveniently hidden away deep within my memory banks. Our idea, and I honestly do not remember who originally came up with it (I don't think I want to claim it), was to design an emblem, having it embroidered and placed on the backs of matching jackets. I don't know for sure, but it may have been to signify our unity. That could be questionable. We wanted to be a club, not a gang. We never intended to become a gang. That would not have been cool in any way. We were absolutely a social club, and our matching jackets told the world who we were.

We hung out together, partied a little, and walked around, trying to look tough. You might ask how that differed from being a gang. Try to avoid asking those tough questions, but, in any case, we never got into any trouble. We sure looked good, and we had to have impressed somebody somewhere for all the money we spent on those stupid jackets! Now I am thinking about the name we gave ourselves, which I would also not have remembered without help. We called ourselves "Sir Guys." If that's not the dumbest name in the world, I don't know what is. I am only guessing now, but perhaps "Sir" was to demand respect, and "Guys" to indicate we were a real, down-to-earth people. I may have even been wearing that cool jacket when I flipped over the back of the couch. My friends must have coerced me into belonging to that club. The thought that it might have been my own idea is too disturbing even to think about. The club itself was a great success. It's the whole idea of it that was a failure. Yeah, well, per usual, moving right along.

There is probably a lengthy string of adjectives that might describe my personality while growing up. Which adjectives one might select may be a matter of who is assembling that string. Way back in junior high school I was very active in sports, and, therefore, some may have described me as something of a jock. Right, "jock" is not an adjective, but jocks don't know any better. At the same time, my academic record was not horrible. No one ever mistook me for a genius, but then I was not a total flunky either. I actually did enjoy my studies in nearly all subjects, particularly English and my foreign languages, which included Latin and German. For that reason, and, of course, the fact that I actually made book covers for all of my books, some people actually had the audacity to call me a nerd. Some of those book covers I did not actually make; I bought some of them, but most I made from grocery store paper shopping bags. Come on though! I could not have been a nerd. After all, I did become an Army, infantry, airborne Ranger and a wounded Vietnam veteran. What kind of a nerd would have done that? My wife calls me a nerd nevertheless, mostly because of the book covers I made, and, I suppose, the fifty-two volumes of the Great Books of the Western World, which my mother bought for me while in high school, and I actually did read most of them, at least in part, if not completely through.

By the way, I also enjoyed writing in my youth, even though, as indicated earlier, I did not always write according to the directions. See, that proves I was not a nerd. Nerds always follow directions, right? Right. Well, anyway, I had at least two very successful writing accomplishments. One was an essay I wrote for a contest, and I actually came in as first place winner. I titled that one "The Fatal Plunge," depicting a skydiving adventure that did not work out well for the jumper, me.

I am not at all sure I can actually count that contest, however, because I have always thought it was my first experience with scammers. I never saw the first place prize, which was supposed to have been glider lessons. That would have been one of the most spectacular things that ever happened to me, because I had always wanted to fly. Gee, do you think that might have caused some minor disappointment for me? For a very brief time, I thought I was a real hotshot. After notification of winning the contest and the first place prize, however, I never heard from them again. I have no idea why I never pursued that. Possibly being sixteen or seventeen years old might have had something to do with it.

The second success was writing a short piece for the school district literary magazine, called Quest. That piece was titled "A Day in the Life of an Amoeba." The editors actually liked it, accepted it and published it in the magazine. Based upon that, I supposed I should never have been referring to myself as an unpublished writer. I was a published author before leaving high school. It was a bit of a creative challenge to establish a voice and point of view of an amoeba. Having such a simple mind might account for my being able to think like an amoeba. It seemed at the time very natural for me.

Chapter 2 – Adventurous and Challenging Youth

Long before high school, my mind was directed and focused, and, as I previously indicated, there was nothing in the world that would ever change my plan for the future. Well, nothing I could see on the horizon at that time could have changed it. Life, however, now and then does throw us a few fastballs and tricky curves with which we never seem to connect. At about sixteen years old, I found it necessary to move closer to the front of my classrooms in order to read the writing on the chalkboards. I could see the "writing on the walls" (sorry, but I was unable to pass that one up), because my eyesight was obviously worsening. I had become near-sighted, and that was not a good thing for Air Force flight school, which has always required perfect vision. There I was, the kid with no contingency plan. My focus was on that one objective, and I had no idea which direction to turn. I was devastated and confused as to what to do next.

Throughout my high school years, the idea of a military life never left me. I began my sophomore year at Mount Miguel High School in Spring Valley, California. The school did not have a junior Army R.O.T.C. program, but did have a Civil Air Patrol program, sponsored by the Air Force. I enjoyed that, but for some reason it just did not appeal to me as much as I thought the Army program would. As it turned out, the next year I transferred to San Diego High School, which did have a junior Army R.O.T.C. program. I remained with the R.O.T.C. program until graduation. I did very well with that. I was on the color guard, as well as our precision drill team. Because I did not go into a third year of that program, I was not eligible to become a cadet officer. However, I did make it to the position of company first sergeant, the highest cadet rank that a second-year student could achieve. It was bittersweet, and I could live with that.

The highlights of my high school years included some very significant adrenaline rushes, and some things, which were substantial motivations to continue with my military plans, whatever they were to be, and wherever they might direct me. Our drill team always had an invitation to march in the big Thanksgiving Day parade in El Cajon, CA, which was a very exciting, televised event. I had a special position on the drill team. Because I was one of the shortest members of the team, and, of course, one of the sharpest (in all modesty), I was selected to be the focus of one of our routines, called "Odd Man Out." Now and then, I shared the position with another short friend and member of the team, who was perhaps even a little sharper than I was. He also had a tough time staying humble.

The idea behind that routine was that the "odd man" would make a wrong turn and march in the opposite direction of the rest of the team, which would require the unit to halt in place, including the odd man. I would be about thirty feet behind while two other members were dispatched to march back, pick me up by both arms and return me to my original position at the end of the unit. It was a very clever maneuver, and we always got a great response from the audience, wherever we performed.

Being on the color guard was equally rewarding. Just as the drill team, we also frequently marched in parades, competed in school competitions, usually winning, and always marched up the center of the football field at all home football games. To present the colors and listen to the National Anthem was always thrilling. We felt like we were a major part of all the activities on campus, and it was great just being out there. Because most of the junior R.O.T.C. programs have disappeared from high school campuses throughout the country, we seldom see those kinds of activities anymore.

I think I developed strong feelings of patriotism I was probably not even aware of at the time. There was a time when President John F. Kennedy was visiting the city, and we (our R.O.T.C. color guard) were acting as part of the hosts at the event. I had a chance to shake the President's hand as he was passing through. That was an honor, and it too made me feel special. There was also a luncheon for the city mayor in which we were very much involved and for which we all received an award. All of those things attributed to my wanting a military career, and those feelings just intensified with time.

My writing experiences continued, as one would expect, through high school, and it was in my sophomore year of high school when my English class had a term paper assignment. That, in and of itself, was not disturbing to me. I enjoyed writing. It was also an interesting year, in that my English teacher, Mrs. Alward, just happened to be my mother's English teacher twenty-five years earlier. On the day she assigned topics for the paper, she read the list of potential topics from which we could choose. Most did not seem particularly interesting to me until she read the topic of "euthanasia." "Youth in Asia" sounded like something, which I would enjoy immensely. I raised my hand and had my topic. I was ready for this.

I began my research right away and worked at it day and night for weeks. It was not as easy as I thought it would be, but, when it was time to turn it in, I had a 5,000-word paper of which I was very proud. It was by far the most massive paper I had ever written, and I thought I had done a very good job of it. I was on hold for a long time before she returned it, and, when she did, she had a very peculiar grin on her face, and one I could only interpret as disbelief. This dummy had interpreted the topic of euthanasia as youth in Asia. Hey, how was I to know? I had never heard the term euthanasia, and it certainly sounded reasonable to me. She never did give me the topic in written form. The assignment was verbal. As it turned out, she did see the humor in it and gave me the benefit of the doubt. I ended up getting a B on the paper, and I was thankful for that. Of course, upon turning it in, I was thinking I had deserved an A. It could have been much worse. I never knew whether she liked my mother as a student or not. I was better off never knowing, I think. Was that failure? Yes. Was it a success? Yes. What more can I say?

Following high school graduation, I attended San Diego State College where, as my cousin's boyfriend did, I went into the Air Force R.O.T.C. program. Although I did quite well with that program, again becoming a member of their drill team, I did not do nearly as well with the academic portion of my curriculum. My heart was not into my academics as much as it should have been. Being very conscious of the fact that I could not fly in the Air Force, and yet knowing very well I needed a college degree, the idea of the military was always on my mind, but I was still without a specific goal. I was without a direction for which to strive. That state of mind is not a key to success.

All through high school, and even through college, I worked every summer to generate additional cash flow. I always wanted to be as little a financial drain on my mother as possible. One of my jobs was flipping hamburgers at Jack-in-the-Box Drive-Thru. I was very good at that. I could knock out thirty hamburgers at a time in five or six minutes. Throwing in a dozen tacos might take a little longer. In a couple of months, I advanced to assistant manager. I went from a dollar an hour to a whopping dollar-ten an hour. Wow, that definitely changed my life style!

I also worked in a bait and tackle shop for a couple of summers, as it was a part of the marina where my mother was a bookkeeper in the office. I also loved that work, even though I had to be on the job every day at 3:00 A.M. There were a few drawbacks to that job, however, besides the starting time. I packaged all sorts of bait, including live anchovies, razor clams, mussels, bloodworms and pile worms. The worms were the most challenging. Both types could grab you in a split second with their claw-like hooks surrounding their mouths while trying to bag them for the fishing consumers in the morning.

Man, when those worms got you, you knew it. The victim of one of their bites would bleed as though punctured by an ice pick. I really disliked that part of the job, having been a victim of those critters many times over, and I tried to warn any unaware anglers of the hazards of baiting their hooks. I recommended running the fishhook through the mouth of the worm, and that way the worm could not get you with his own hooks. That could almost ruin a good fishing day before it ever got started.

Another summer job I had was with a friend of my mother. He owned a small airline, which ran flights from

San Diego to Catalina Island. All of his planes were amphibians. I helped with baggage and loading it on the aircraft. It was an interesting job, and it paid well, and, when my birthday rolled around, my boss sent me, with my girlfriend at the time, off to Catalina Island for the day. We had a great day, and it did not cost us a dime.

The same man who owned the airline also owned a mountain resort up in the High Sierras, northeast of Fresno, California. He invited my mother and me to work at the resort the following summer, and we took him up on the offer. My mother worked in the office, and I worked in the general store, which also had a butcher shop in the back. Another job was to help with the campfires we had every night. It was a great summer job, and I loved everything about it, including meeting a very nice young lady whose company I very much enjoyed for the whole summer.

Every job seems to have a few drawbacks, and this one was no exception. One day a woman came into the shop and wanted some sliced ham. I did not have much experience in the butcher shop, but I was more than willing to slice some ham for her. I went to the back, grabbed the ham and a knife, and began to slice away. Now, the knives in a butcher shop are for good reason razor sharp. Rather than slicing the ham half-way through and flipping it over to continue the cut, which would seem the most reasonable and logical method, I chose the road less taken, and ran the knife underneath the ham and up around the ham bone. Unfortunately, my thumb was also in line with the knife blade. The blade went right through ham and thumb, all the way to the thumb bone. Ouch! I proceeded to bleed all over the ham and everything around it, and the customer, to my knowledge, never got her ham that day. My mother rushed me down the mountain to the nearest hospital to stitch up my wound. I did not seem to be completely through with my accidents.

As a side, I really should elaborate a bit about my and my mother's previous employer. His name was Jack. I'm quite sure he is long dead by now. I mentioned he owned the small airline that made runs to Catalina. He was actually a very difficult man for whom to work. He always seemed to have an attitude, and very seldom did he ever wear a warm, friendly smile. He had the perpetual chip on his shoulder. There may well have been good, though possibly not justifiable, reasons for that attitude. He was missing most of both legs. He was in a wheelchair all the time, and life was very tough for him.

Many years prior to the time I knew him, Jack was on a flight, piloting the aircraft to Catalina Island, and in the process of landing on the water, when one of the propellers of his two-engine plane came loose, cutting straight through the cockpit, severing both legs well above the knees. I always had the feeling he would rather have lost his life, rather than his two legs. It would seem that he was one who was willing to take risks, but not willing to accept consequences if things went wrong. I can only hope I am not in that category.

During my early years of college, I had a lack of motorized transportation to go to and from school. I bought myself a very nice ten-speed bicycle, since it was about seven miles out to the college campus from where I lived. I had two incidents during my morning and evening bicycle trips, both of which left me with lasting memories. My bicycle looked much like many I later saw in Southeast Asia, though maybe a bit nicer, only because it was usually stacked with as much junk as I could get aboard, mostly books for all my classes for the day.

I was riding down El Cajon Boulevard one day when suddenly a car door flew open right in front of me. I had no time to react. My bike smashed right into the door, and I flew over my handlebars, as well as the car door, landing in the street on my back. I was not feeling great, but, surprisingly, I was not injured either. I thought about getting up right away, and then my evil side spoke to me. I decided to pay back a little of what I had received.

I am generally not a vindictive person, but that particular time I was extremely angry. I could not believe the guy had just flung his door open without even looking behind him. I was not ready to let him off quite that easily. I just decided to lie on my back in the street, as though unconscious. The man was terribly upset by what he had done, but, of course, I was not quite satisfied he had paid his debt. At last, I began to feel his pain as well as my own, and I got up and just glared at him. He helped me find all my books that were scattered all over the street and made sure I was all right. My guess is he would be more careful from that point on. What was the big "silver lining" behind that cloud? It was probably that he learned a lesson in looking out for others, and I learned a little more about how vulnerable I was to the outside world.

The second bicycle mishap was on my way home from school one night, as I did have one night class at the time, and it was well after dark before the class let out. I was riding down the one big hill on my trip, part of College Avenue. The down slope went for about a quarter of a mile before going uphill again. I liked to get up to a good forty-five miles per hour going down that hill to make it easier for the upward trek following it. There had apparently been some construction work done on the road that day, and there was a square hole cut in the road about eighteen inches on each side and about six inches deep. The workers had not marked the hole before leaving for the day. Guess who found it. Right. My front wheel hit the hole at the highest speed and with such impact it tossed me again over the handlebars and into the street.

My body and my books slid about thirty feet down the street. My books did not fare well, decreasing in value for selling them back to the bookstore, and my body was not much better with bruises and skid marks that lasted for a very long time. The front wheel and tire of the bike were history, with a dented rim looking like a pie with a piece cut out of it. I carried the front end of the bike as I walked the remaining six miles home that evening, after having spent a half hour in the dark trying to locate all of my damaged books with a rather broken body that was in a good deal of pain. That was a true lesson in humility, and I was, at least for a short time, thinking about bringing a lawsuit against the city of San Diego. I was just not, by any stretch, a happy camper, but it did encourage me to work harder to buy a new car, which I did shortly thereafter. Because I limped away from that little incident, I do consider it a success. It could have been a lot worse. At that time in my life, just living day to day was a risky business.

Because of my high school Junior Army R.O.T.C. program and having been on the color guard and drill team, I became part of the San Diego State College Air Force R.O.T.C. drill team. We frequently traveled the country on drill team competitions. In my second year of college, we had a scheduled competition in Salt Lake City, Utah, and the team was geared up and ready to go. The day before departure, we found out the Air Force could only give us one aircraft, rather than the two requested. Only half the team could go. The other half was to stay behind with explicit instructions not to travel on our own up to Salt Lake City, as neither the Air Force nor the college would accept responsibility.

Well, that was like waving a red flag for most of us young men. Four of us, probably the biggest risk-takers, packed up and headed out in one of the team members' cars. After driving all Friday night, we arrived early Saturday, the morning of the competition, only to find out the rest of the team never made it, due to engine problems with the aircraft. That was a wasted trip, and we were not terribly interested in seeing the competition without our own team being there. We decided just to head back home to San Diego. I had tried to sleep on the way up to Salt Lake City while one of the others drove. On the way back, I volunteered to do the night driving because I could never seem to sleep in a moving vehicle. That was probably a bad decision. Sure enough, I tried to sleep during the day, and could not for the life of me. We made a short stop in Las Vegas, and I drove from there.

After several hours, we were well into California, approaching Barstow. I began to feel the drowsiness coming on, and actually did stop at one point to shut my eyes for a while. I could not sleep and started out again. It was a cold night, and no one would condone open windows. I could not find a decent radio station to keep me alert. All I could find was the equivalent of elevator music, just the kind to lull you to sleep. Everything seemed to be working against me.

The distance between Barstow and San Bernardino, California is about ninety miles, and I do not remember a thing between those two towns. I must have been at least half-asleep the whole way. Close to San Bernardino, I felt rough road under my tires, which meant I was drifting off to the right side of the road. I woke up, and at the same time my friend, riding shotgun (passenger side) and the owner of the car, woke up and panicked. He reached over, grabbed the steering wheel and turned it heavily to the left. That put the car heading right into on-coming traffic. That would never do; so, I pulled it back to the right.

Pulling the wheel to the right sent the car into a side skid until it hit the raised portion of the side of the road, flipping it over about three times, as it rolled down an embankment and into a ditch about fifteen feet deep. The car was a convertible, and the top had torn off completely when the car had settled upright on all four wheels. The two of us in the front seat were still in place, but when I looked into the back seat, the other two were gone! The first thing that went through my mind was that I had just killed two of my friends. Things looked grim.

I got out and began to look around for my missing friends. I found one of them with one of his legs appearing to be pinned under the car, but it really was not. He had a mild concussion and a dislocated hip, but was otherwise all right. The other had flown through the air and landed in some bushes, and he was uninjured.

In the meantime, I felt a little tickle on my face and reached up to wipe it, and discovered my hand was covered with blood. I had not felt a thing, but my face had apparently made some heavy contact with the steering column, which left me with a radial fracture and fifty-seven stitches. Hey, we probably all should have been dead. We were more than just lucky. My guardian angels were still on the job, and maybe a few for the other guys as well. What seemed after Salt Lake City to be a complete failure was actually a significant success; a risk that worked out reasonably well. Nobody died, and that is always a good thing. Logically I should have killed us all.

For more than five years I had been struggling with what my goals in life should be. What was it I really wanted to do? I could not find the answers to that dilemma, and I had very little effective guidance, from either home or elsewhere. There is very little more frustrating than having a very specific goal for your life, watching it die, and not having a clue what the next step should be. I was not completely over the idea of going into the Air Force, but to go into that branch of service with no intention of flying made no sense to me. Doing that would be like going into the Army and not being part of one of the combat arms (infantry, armor and artillery). I do have great respect for all who serve faithfully in the combat support and combat service support areas of the Army. Those areas of service just do not happen to be for me. With that much determined, I had a good idea of what I did not want, and that was helpful. I could at least narrow the field of consideration a great deal at that point.

I have not always attained the highest level of performance possible in everything I have ever attempted, but that has always been my objective, and it always will be. That is just who I am. Continuing my thoughts about the Air Force, my second idea was to go into weather, becoming a meteorologist. I knew that was a very significant part of the Air Force, and even though I still would not ever pilot an aircraft, I might still be able to be in the air a good deal of the time, and the elements of the weather have always intrigued me. That field did require, however, a good deal of math, not really my best "suit" or my favorite subject. While in college, I progressed up to calculus and analytic geometry, whereupon I crashed big time. I had not come even close to finishing that course before I felt the necessity to drop it, as well as the idea of meteorology. Having to drop that math class once again felt like I had met with another failure. There I was again: the man without a plan.

Even before those problems with math were taking their toll on me, I was finishing my second year of college, and just barely making it, remaining on academic probation. I went into my third year at San Diego State College, and continued the struggle to stay "alive" academically. The year was 1965, and the month was October. I was walking down the street somewhere in San Diego, when I looked up, and right there, staring me in the face, was a US Army recruiting station! My first thought was, "Holy guacamole! What in the world am I doing standing in front of this place?" However

(Oh, there's that word again, just as bad as but), I had a very strange feeling I was in the right place at the right time.

I "walked right in and sat right down" (to quote a few words from an old Wanda Jackson song), and a whole new life began for me from that moment. I signed on the old dotted line, and I then belonged to "Uncle Sam." Oh, crap! My next chore was to go home and inform my parents. It did catch my mother and stepfather a little off guard, but they were extremely understanding, as well as extremely worried, knowing me, and the fact that there was a war kicking up in Southeast Asia.

The worst of my mother's fears had come true. I had voluntarily gone into the infantry! Everyone thought I had lost my marbles, but my decision was exactly what I wanted, and I also expected to go into Officer Candidate School (OCS) to attain a commission. That, too, was something of a risk, as there was no guarantee that would even happen. I first had to pass exams to qualify for OCS, which fortunately I did. Beyond that, I still had no plan, but that decision put in place a pattern for my life that has lasted up until the present, and that was nearly fifty years ago. I have never had regrets about it. All right, Vietnam was not always a great deal of fun, but it was a very significant part of my life, which helped develop me into who I am today.

Chapter 3 – Military Training

Bidding adieu to my parents, I departed San Diego by Greyhound bus to Los Angeles, with an overnight stay there, and then boarded a jet, bound for Fort Polk, Louisiana for my basic training. For every person who has ever been through any military basic training, his or her version of that experience will differ from that of just about anyone else. In fact, each branch of the service has a different style of basic training, and all branches of the service, except the Army, refer to it as boot camp. I will, therefore, try to remember to refer to it by that name.

Most people would agree the Marines probably have the toughest program for boot camp, followed by the Army, and then the Navy, Coast Guard and Air Force, not all of the latter necessarily in that order. The different perceptions are probably due to the amount of stress each person can take at any given time, as well as how much stress that particular program exerts on the trainees. What you or I might consider a proverbial "piece of cake" might be one of the worst experiences ever encountered for another person. Each of us can be the only accurate judge of our own experiences.

One thing I will say about my experiences with boot camp is it did leave some lasting impressions on me, as well as some memories, which I will never forget, and not all of them bad. Shortly after arrival at my training company, we were in formation, and the drill sergeant asked if anyone had prior military experience, including any ROTC. Without thinking about it, I raised my hand, and nearly as quickly, my drill sergeant designated me as the leader of my platoon. That turned out to be an interesting development. The composition of my platoon, about thirty-five or forty men, was very scary.

In the 1960s, the Army was a little different than it is today. We had not only a military draft going on, but we also had a policy of recruiting even more into the service by giving those who were going to jail an alternative. It was go to jail or go into the Army. Most of those "gentlemen" decided that serving their country would beat going to jail, even though it meant they also would probably end up in Vietnam. I think the vast majority of those in that category ended up, not only in my company, but also in my platoon.

I had thugs from Los Angeles, New York City, Chicago, Detroit and everywhere else the big gangs congregated. How so many of those wonderful young men managed to find their way into my platoon, I will never know. Most of them were giants compared to me. I have never met the physical qualifications for professional basketball. I was about five feet, six inches tall, and I was their leader. As you can imagine, it was the beginning of some beautiful relationships.

I have always felt confident about dealing with most personality types; however, I do not do attitudes. After my Army active duty and college I was a high school teacher, and I always told my students, "Show me an attitude, and I'll show you the door." In this training situation, I was thinking I would definitely see some attitudes, but was I capable of showing some of them the door, or did I even want to try to go there? If I really wanted to have my butt kicked or much worse, I could go with that plan, but diplomacy, I thought, might be the best way to go. I was sometimes a little on the crazy side, but not a total idiot. My biggest challenges were to make sure we accomplished our missions, met our responsibilities, and did it better than any platoon in the company. That seemed to be setting some extremely high goals, especially for that crew, but I was determined to do just that, "come hell or high water," and sometimes the water did seem to rise beyond the comfort level.

There are probably very few people, if any, who go through any boot camp, graduate and can claim they loved the experience. I have met some who are exceptions to that rule, but the Army did not design their training with that purpose in mind. The whole idea was to prepare the average young civilian person for military life, or at least several years of military regimen. Forty or fifty years ago, the idea was to turn the boys into men, but today we have a very large contingency of women in the military. Today's military should be turning young people into mature adults, or at least giving it a supreme effort. Boot camp is also part of the process of eliminating those not fit for military service.

If young men and women cannot successfully complete boot camp, then they either do the training again or they receive discharges and go home. There are extenuating circumstances for some trainees that will allow them to "recycle" and try it a second time. Many are unsuitable for military service, and the military cannot use them in any way. They may have physical problems previously undetected, they may be unable to take orders well, or they may be unable to deal with the pressures that often come with that type of life. What we all have to understand is that again the military is not for everyone.

My boot camp experiences were relatively easy, when compared to many others who have undergone the same thing. Because of my prior military experience, and being in a leadership position, I had a few privileges most were not able to enjoy. KP (kitchen police) was one of those. I think I only had that duty maybe a half dozen times all the time I was in the Army. There were, of course, a few duties I was expected to accomplish that were above and beyond what others were expected to do. I had to maintain some semblance of order in my platoon, and make sure everyone was where they were supposed to be and doing what they were supposed to be doing at all times. That was a challenge in itself. Of course, making sure they were not doing what they were not supposed to be doing was even more of a challenge.

My cup was full enough without adding all of the smaller chores.

Boot camp was, in fact, a survival situation for me. My job was to ensure all my men were doing their jobs and to do that I had to be assertive, yet try to avoid aggression and becoming offensive. Both diplomacy and psychology would be required if I hoped to be successful with this crew. I had to figure out, with little or no training in such matters, how to make these men get their jobs done, stay out of trouble, and not have them hate me in the process. Finishing boot camp alive and well was a primary goal for me. That was what my greatest challenge became for the next few weeks.

If I had not been able to accomplish my mission and fulfill my responsibilities, I would be forced to go head to head with my drill sergeant, and what a guy he was! He was one of the few people with whom I could physically look eye to eye, as we were about the same height. He was without a doubt one of the meanest people you could ever imagine. At least that is the way he appeared to most people most of the time. His name was Drill Sergeant Moyer, and he was an individual whom no one who ever served under him would ever forget.

When Drill Sergeant Moyer addressed you, he could talk straight through your face. His words would seemingly penetrate your mind, body and soul. I'm not sure today whether or not he had any top teeth, because his upper lip was always snug against his bottom teeth as he spoke, and his words emerged from the spaces through his bottom teeth. If you can imagine an f-word, and he had plenty of those, pronounced with his upper lip pressed against his lower teeth, his breath whisking through the spaces in his teeth, that was the sound. His words may have been somewhat muffled, but there was never any doubt in anyone's mind what he was saying; it was perfectly clear.

Drill Sergeant Moyer also had another side he showed to those to whom he did not always have to be a drill sergeant. He could be soft-spoken, gentle, caring and an honest-to-goodness human being. In essence, he was a great leader, and proved it to those who knew him well. I was one of the few among our trainees who were ever able to get that close to him, and for that, I am thankful. I learned a great deal from that man, and, therefore, I will always be indebted to him.

With regard to our boot camp, it was something of an anomaly, in that, at the same time some of us were trying to stay alive by avoiding killing one another in our training, we were in training in order to learn to stay alive in war, by learning how to kill more effectively. Does that make any sense at all? I didn't think so. The real "kill" training came later, however, in advanced training, particularly if it were to be in the combat arms. The whole idea of Basic Combat Training (BCT) was not to develop real soldiers; that was yet to come. The idea was to "weed out" the "ash and trash" and make soldiers out of the remainder who had at least some chance of success in the military. Let's face the facts; as I've pointed out, some people are just not suited for military life; they cannot deal with that type of structure and discipline. We did eliminate a few, and the remainder made it through the training cycle, and graduated. We did well and were more than successful. We were then soldiers.

From Fort Polk, I went home for a brief Christmas leave and on to Fort Ord, California, right off the Monterey Bay, about a hundred miles south of San Francisco. There I was to do my Infantry Advanced Individual Training (AIT). It has been said that every soldier is first and foremost an infantryman, a fighting man (or woman, although women in the infantry and other combat arms is a very recent phenomenon, still in the experimental stages). To have the distinction of wearing the crossed rifles on his or her uniform, each soldier must have successfully completed the advanced course in infantry. The same concept of an advance course applies to any occupational specialty; it always follows boot camp and is usually about eight weeks long. Each person upon completion will wear a branch insignia.

It seems I always had the mindset for the infantry, but it was here I learned what it was to live the life. After having had the general military foundation set in boot camp, I was now in a total immersion environment with the real infantry. That included training in the weapons of the infantry, the tactics, the map reading, the communications equipment used at the time, and everything we had to know in order to survive. We would also never want to exclude "the spirit of the bayonet!" During bayonet training, the instructor would always yell out, "What's the spirit of the bayonet?" Our answer would follow, "To kill!" I just thought I would enlighten you, just in case you were not aware of that, and in the off chance you might be interested in the Army and the infantry in particular.

After having become "an American fighting man," I was on hold for four or five more months, awaiting my Infantry OCS class. My assignment was to be an "acting jack," whereby I was given slip-on stripes of a buck sergeant (E-5), but was only paid as a Private First Class (E-3). I worked with a training unit, "pushing" troops. It was not real rank, but I did have the privileges of a sergeant, and I enjoyed my job. It was also good leadership training, preceding OCS. I also attended an additional leadership school prior to going off to Fort Benning, Georgia and Infantry OCS. When my class date finally arrived, I was ready for another transition in my military life. I was now bound for "Benning School for Boys," as we affectionately referred to it.

I had prior warning this course was not to be anything resembling a picnic. The next six months proved that an accurate assessment. Rather than drill sergeants, we now had tactical officers, or TAC officers for short. Their jobs were to keep the maximum pressure on at all times, and they were very effective in accomplishing that mission. Some of the TACs we learned to dislike intensely, others we really got to hate. Later, when I heard rumors of one of them being killed in action in Vietnam, I presumed it was not from a hostile force. It had to have been "friendly fire." Later I discovered it was not true anyway. His name was not on the Wall (Vietnam War Memorial in Washington, DC).

It would not have surprised me at all, had a "friendly fire" fatality been true. Some people, when they receive a little authority, allow it to go to their heads. When they are young and inexperienced, they sometimes do not understand how to control that authority. The "power" they seem to feel is accepting responsibility, and not having a clue as to what to do with it. OCS TAC officers were not immune to that condition, and it frequently caused many officers to lose their lives in combat.

Some of those TAC officers actually seemed to have feelings and a controlled level of compassion. Of course, part of their job was to refrain from showing any compassion, and many were excellent at that. A few seemed to enjoy it a little too much. They seemed to find joy in the pain of others, and that is not a healthy way to be; not in a training environment, and absolutely not in a combat environment. To be honest, however, all who have been through it would probably have to agree that the continuous stress placed upon us contributed greatly to our becoming effective leaders and more able to work under intense stress and adverse conditions.

I had some very interesting experiences in that school. Many were educational, physically challenging, emotional (funny, sad, exciting, traumatic, and adventurous), and some were even life changing to a degree. It was a period of six months that developed me as an individual, and directed me into a new lifestyle and mindset. It taught me new ways to deal with people and my environment. Probably for the first time in my life, I really learned what it meant to rely on others for help through difficult times. I learned a whole new concept of camaraderie, and how this entire OCS class, which was a team, differed from any other group of individuals I had ever encountered up to that point in my life.

In the OCS environment, we learned to function under pressure, regardless of what we were doing. There were TAC officers around at all times, not only to monitor what we were doing, but also to intervene and add a little excitement to whatever it was. One example is just sitting down to dinner in the mess hall. I recall one evening, when I entered the mess hall, I went through the line for my food and proceeded to sit down to enjoy a good meal.

There were a few rules in OCS that are a bit different from most units in the Army, and all branches of the service have similar rules for their officer training programs. One rule was you had to sit at attention, and square off your bites while eating. You could not eat too slowly, because you would then be on casual status, acting as though you had all night to eat. You could not eat too quickly, or you would be a "pig." There had to be a perfect balance there, and, of course, the TAC officers were there to make sure that a balance would seldom occur.

That particular evening I went through the chow line and sat down to enjoy my meal. After two or three bites, one of the TAC officers yelled across the dining hall, directing his comment to me, "Candidate McClarren, you are eating entirely too slowly! Eat and get the hell out of my dining facility!" I answered, "Yes, sir!" and proceeded to put a rush on that meal, as I was determined to finish it. Two more bites and he yelled again in my direction, "Candidate McClarren! You are a pig! Give me twenty laps around the mess hall." I jammed one more bite down as I headed toward the door, but not before dropping for twenty push-ups for taking that last bite. Upon returning from my laps and sitting down to finish my meal, the TAC looked over and said, "Candidate, you have been in my mess hall entirely too long. Dinner is over. Get the hell out of here!"

That was the end of my evening nourishment. I was off to bigger and better things. I had become immune to all of that nonsense harassment. We all reached a point at which we hardly noticed it anymore. I also developed a special attitude where what bothered many others did not really bother me as much. The way I saw it was nothing they could do or say to me would change my life in any way, at least not for the worse. If anything, it could help. They had their job to do, and I had mine.

There were times when many of my fellow candidates experienced heavy stress for any number of reasons. Some would gather together upstairs and break a few of the rules, only one of which was ordering pizza after hours. After lights out, no one was even supposed to be awake, let alone up and roaming around. Frequently I would be in the latrine in a shower stall shining my boots way after lights were out. If a TAC were to catch you doing something like that, it would not go well. I ended up in the TAC office in the "dying cockroach" position in front of the TAC officer's desk on more than one occasion. It was sometimes necessary to be up after hours, as we just did not have time during the day to get everything accomplished. It was through such opportunities we were taught to budget our time. They trained us well through rather harsh consequences for not doing it well the first time.

Once, some of my peers, and I honestly was not one of them, decided that it was time to order out for pizza. We all ended up paying dearly for it, and I do not mean financially. It was quite late that night when some of them took the initiative to make a call to the local pizza parlor. They arranged to rendezvous with the delivery person, without alerting the on-duty TAC officer. After linking up with the delivery person, they took the pizza and drinks up to the roof of the barracks to pig out. Upon finishing, the idiots left the boxes and drink cups up on the roof without disposing of them.

The TAC officer on duty must have become suspicious because he began to investigate. He went up to the roof and made the discovery. At approximately 3:00 A.M. the loudest thrashing of a trash can you can imagine rousted us out of our racks with a half dozen TAC officers screaming at the tops of their lungs for us to be up, dressed in freshly starched fatigues and spit-shined boots, and out in formation in three minutes. We were well aware that we were in for trouble, but had no idea how much and most of us for what reason.

We were out in formation, on time and looking sharp. We actually thought we were ready for them. Wrong! The first thing we did was drop for a thousand or so push-ups (possibly some exaggeration). Finally, the TACs allowed us to stand up, when we had little or no feeling left in our arms, and definitely no strength. We then dropped to our bellies onto the asphalt parking lot and started crawling. We low-crawled for a quarter of a mile or more to the local branch of the Chattahoochee River. After we had submerged into the river and remained there for a while, we crawled back to the barracks parking lot, still soaking wet, muddy, and our highly spit-shined boots thrashed. About forty years later, the country song "Way Down Yonder On the Chattahoochee" had a great deal of meaning to me. It became near and dear to my heart. The fond memories never stop.

When they released us to go back into the barracks, we found the other TACs had ransacked the place. They knocked over bunks, overturned footlockers, and turned the whole building into a disaster area. We had to shower and get ready for the day, as well as putting everything back together for an inspection later. There was no time for going back to bed. The bottom line is we were not at all happy with our "compadres" who were the perpetrators of the pizza pandemonium. They were the risk takers and we all paid the price.

The above incident is just one example of our being a single, cohesive group. If a few people found trouble, we all accepted responsibility. We did everything together. We ate, slept, worked, studied and suffered together. There is virtually no end to what we seemed to have in common. In essence, we bonded in our unity. There are few working or social groups in civilian life that compare to that type of support group. Exceptions might include law enforcement and public safety organizations. Camaraderie develops, most particularly within military units, and especially in wartime scenarios. It has to be that way in order for units to function properly and be successful in combat. Each individual must add to the whole body, such that the body can function as a single entity.

Another environment where camaraderie proved to be even more important to me than OCS was Ranger School. That is by far the toughest school the US Army has to offer. It is the equivalent of the Navy Seals but primarily oriented to land operations. The whole idea is to put people through special operations training, and insure each student is under intense stress at all times. It is very effective. Sometimes the specific risks that Ranger School students take are more by chance than by choice. One specific incident always comes to mind, which occurred during our initial three-week Benning phase (at Fort Benning, GA), and, if you have previously read my MILITARY LIFE SERVICE OR CAREER - A SOLDIER'S PERSPECTIVE, you will have already read this story, but it is important here to relate the message. Anyway, we woke up each morning at 4:00 A.M., fell out for PT, went on our four-mile run, and then negotiated the obstacle course. Showers would follow that routine and then breakfast. Finally, it would be time to begin the academic portion of the day.

The obstacle course one particular morning remains vivid for me today. It began with the wire obstacle, whereby we had to crawl or scoot on our backs through six or eight inches of very wet and slushy mud (Georgia red clay) under a barbed wire mesh. After negotiating that simple obstacle, we went to the parallel ladder. That consisted of thirteen rungs across a trench full of water, about four feet deep. The object was to "hang free" with both hands on the first rung, feet hanging straight down, and then move forward hand-over-hand to the other side, climb down, and be off to the next obstacle.

When the lane grader gave the initial command to "hang free," not having heard him, I was still in the mounting position with my left foot on the block. The lane grader glared at me and yelled, "You, cheater, I said, 'Hang free!'" I then dropped off the block, hanging with both feet freely suspended. Upon command, I began to negotiate the ladder. It was a very simple chore for me. I had excellent upper body strength, and thirteen rungs were the proverbial "piece of cake." As I approached the end of the ladder, the lane grader yelled at me again, "You, cheater, turn around and go back!"

Upon rolling my eyes, I turned around and headed back to the start. Each time I was close to reaching the end, the lane grader addressed me the same way and gave me the same directions. After a good ten minutes of this repetition, I was beginning to tire just a little. I was on what may have been the end of my endurance, and about half way to the end of the rungs, when the lane grader gave his final command: "Drop, cheater!"

I stopped, released my grip, and dropped into the pitch-black water below. It appeared black, because it was still dark out at that hour of the morning. I then struggled to the end of the trench whereby I attempted to drag myself out of the water. I was wet and muddy, and there was a rubber mat at the end of which, if I had been tall enough, I could have grabbed hold and pulled myself from the water. My five-foot-six-inch stature was a bit short of that being an easy task. After five or six attempts at jumping and sliding back down the slimy mat into the water, having nearly exhausted the remainder of my energy, I managed to grasp the edge of the mat and pull myself out. The next command I heard ordered me to low-crawl to the next obstacle.

The next obstacle was a construction of logs about twenty-five feet high, over which I had to crawl. That was relatively easy, even being totally exhausted. From there, I crawled to the final obstacle, a rope climb. There was a twenty-five-foot rope suspended over the center of a square pool of water. The pool was about fifteen feet on each side, which meant I would have to jump approximately seven and a half feet to grasp the rope, and then make the climb to the top.

The first challenge was simply to leap through the air and grab the rope. Easy enough, right? I sized up the situation. How far do I have to jump? At exactly what point do I have to seize the rope? What hand and eye coordination do I need for this little trick? I had it all together. I took the giant leap, sailed directly toward the rope, and my hands came together just at the right time. Unfortunately, what they grasped was not rope, but rather thin air, each hand passing by the other. My body remained suspended in the air for a split second, just long enough to say quietly to myself, "Shit!" just before plunging into the water, which again was about four feet deep.

From that point, I had another significant challenge. There was a knot tied at the bottom of the rope, which was just within my reach. I needed to pull myself up high enough to get my feet on top of the knot, thus gaining another five feet so I could pull with both my arms and legs to make my way to the top of the rope. I just had to make it far enough up that rope to grab the second rope, which ran from the top of the center rope I was on, back down to the outer edge of the pool. From the top, all I had to do was slide down, and the task would be complete.

It was all I could do to keep moving upward, as my hands were wet, and it was tough just getting a good grip on the rope, and the little strength I had left in my arms was fading rapidly. Inch by inch I came closer to the top. When I was not more than two feet from the top, I had expended all that I had. I could not get another inch of elevation. Suddenly I just released the rope, screaming, "Aaaahhh!" all the way down until I embraced the water once again.

I resurfaced, looked around to get my bearings and headed to the edge of the pool. It was tough, but I managed again to pull myself from the water. I then headed toward the barracks for my shower, breakfast, which I believe was humble pie, and I was then ready to begin my normal academic day. Most days were not a great deal different from that one, but that day did create a memory. It taught me a good lesson in self-discipline, endurance and dealing with stress, in addition to humility. I just chalked it up as another growing experience. What would life be without those little gems?

Life at Ranger School presented a variety of wonderful experiences and memories. One memory I will carry with me forever is our motivational seventeen-mile road "march." I put the word march in quotation marks, as that term could be misleading. I was probably the shortest person in my ranger company, and the individual leading the march was a very tall and lanky second lieutenant. All of us, except for the lieutenant of course, were loaded with full field packs, carrying rifles and wearing steel pots. He was wearing a light uniform, a soft cap and a pistol belt with a canteen. He could walk faster than I could run. Consequently, for me, the seventeen-mile road march was a seventeen-mile run.

After the first three miles, I had blisters on both heels. I came to a point, probably ten miles into the march (run), whereby I became dizzy and began to see white spots dancing around in front of my eyes. My "ranger buddies" noticed I was not looking very good and came to my rescue, which was totally against the rules at the school. Two of them, one on each side, recognized what was going on even before I did. One of them grabbed my rifle, and the other supported me by grabbing one of my arms. After no more than a minute or less I regained my composure, my dizziness went away, and my strength returned. I grabbed my rifle, and finished the march.

All was well at the end, except for the massive blisters on both of my heels, which had peeled off completely, leaving nothing but raw meat and two boots full of blood. Oh, that was indeed a character builder and an exercise in physical endurance. I had made it all the way and felt good about it mentally, if not physically, and that was the important thing. That was another good example of building a sense of camaraderie. What those men did for me was totally against Ranger School policy, and they could have been in a great deal of trouble for doing it. They were willing to take that risk for me, and I certainly appreciated it. It strengthened our relationship immeasurably. There was also the unwritten rule, of course, that the student rangers were a team, and a teammate would never allow a ranger buddy to fail at what he was doing if there were any way to avoid it. In my case it worked.

I, just as most people, have undergone a number of disappointments throughout my life, but there is one example in particular that stands out way beyond all the others, and that one is tied directly to Ranger School. The school at the time, and I know nothing of any recent changes, had a policy of placing all students into one of three categories at the conclusion of the course. Each had either "not successfully completed the course," "successfully completed the course," or "successfully completed the course and awarded the distinguished ranger tab." The latter category is that for which all strive, and the majority actually do achieve. The criteria for the award of the ranger tab include being in charge of and passing three out of five simulated combat patrols. That would indicate the patrol leader (student) would have successfully negotiated the route, reached the correct objective at the correct time, and been completely successful overall in the opinions of the lane graders.

I found myself in an unfortunate situation, whereby I had not exactly won the affections of my lane graders, and their criteria for grading were quite subjective. I had already had nearly a year as an infantry platoon leader in Vietnam, and my rank while I was going through Ranger School was captain, although theoretically no one had any rank in that school. The lane graders, all NCO's, knew all of the ranger students and their ranks. The fact that they knew I was a captain was of no benefit to me whatsoever. They were not about to cut me any slack, not that I wanted any special favors. I just wanted to have equal and fair treatment. I was never convinced that ever happened.

I was unable to complete a couple of the missions successfully, due to unavoidable complications. The remainder should have all been successful, but somehow my lane graders did fail me on a couple more of them, including two make-ups. I apparently did not meet their standards, and did not receive "the distinguished Ranger tab." That was a very "bitter pill to swallow," but one I survived and I am, for the most part, all right with it today. I still have not extinguished all of that bitter taste however.

The Ranger School students had two ways to return to Fort Benning from Florida. Those who were awarded the Ranger tab were flown back to Georgia, and those who did not receive the tab were loaded up on "cattle" trucks and driven back to Georgia. The faculty did seem to be making a point to those who did not qualify for the tab. Not only did we have to suffer the pains of successfully completing the course without receiving the tab, but we also had to have the full impact of the staff attitudes in order to make us feel even worse. They really knew how to make it hurt. I have to admit I had a tough time with that element. I include that experience in my list of lessons learned, and as another aspect of character development. We must always be able to see some of the positive elements around what appears to be gloom. They are there. We just have to have our eyes wide open to see them.

Covering Ranger School was a bit out of chronological order, but it was on a similar subject and, therefore, seemed to fit in. However, getting back to the final days of OCS, my classmates and I finally reached graduation and received commissions as second lieutenants. Those of us who successfully completed the course were off to begin our new lives as commissioned officers in the US Army. On the one hand, being US Army officers was great, and that was by far the most important thing in our minds. The down side was most of us knew exactly what our primary destination was going to be from the day of graduation, and that was not great news for most of us, though certainly expected.

Being newly commissioned infantry officers, very few of us were not going off to Vietnam in the very near future. The norm would be for most of us to have a training unit assignment somewhere for six months, just to get some experience as an officer, and then it would be off to Southeast Asia to get the feel of a real infantry officer in combat. It was a risk we all voluntarily took; so, there was certainly no one on whom to place blame but ourselves. From that point on, it was, "Good luck, Charlie."

Chapter 4 – US Army, Vietnam

I was no exception to the norm for infantry second lieutenants. My first assignment as an officer was to a basic training company at Fort Polk, Louisiana for the next six months, and then off to the Canal Zone in Panama for The Jungle Operations Course (JOC), which seemed to be a prerequisite for most infantry officers assigned to units in Vietnam. That was a very interesting and enjoyable course, but one I later referred to as a "gentleman's course." The only requirement was to complete two weeks of training and each student received an award, which identified him as a Jungle Expert. Really? Give me a break. Two weeks in the jungles of Panama and you are a "jungle expert"? Right. Like that really happened. After a few months in the jungles of Vietnam, you might be a little closer to it, but designating a soldier as a jungle expert after that lame two-week course was a misnomer if I ever saw one and a delusion on someone's part. Granted, some of you may have gone through the same school and have different opinions, and even had slightly different experiences, but "that's my story, and I'm stickin' to it."

I returned from Panama to pick up my new orders reassigning me to a replacement battalion somewhere in the Republic of Vietnam. I went home for a quick leave before my departure, and I was off to my Southeast Asian adventure, an all-expenses-paid trip, and complements of the United States Army. Prior to that departure, however, I had become very close to the sister of one of my OCS classmates, who happened to live only a hundred miles or so north of San Diego, in the Los Angeles area. I had fallen head over heels for her, and I was absolutely in love. It was the real thing.

As wonderful and real as that love was, it lasted long enough for me to get on the airplane headed west from San Francisco. I must have written her ten letters in a matter of a few weeks. I may have gotten one or two letters answered, as some of my letters home seem to indicate, but I actually do not recall receiving anything from her. Is love not a beautiful thing? I know it took at least a week or two to get over that relationship. She really was hot, but the relationship seemed to cool very quickly. I believe that is called "life in the big city." Right? I think I also gained a deeper understanding of the distinction between falling in love and falling in lust.

All right, I was on my journey, a flight of about nineteen hours from San Francisco. We were to stop over for refueling at Wake Island, east of the Philippines, and then on to Vietnam. We were aboard an Air Force C-141, the newest and fastest Air Force cargo jet of the time, and, because it was a standard cargo plane, the seats were reversed so we flew facing backwards for nineteen hours. We could have ended up in Europe for all we knew. It would have been preferable, but no such luck. It turned out to be more than just a little interesting even before our arrival at our destination.

The pilot had informed us shortly after leaving Travis Air Force Base, just north of San Francisco, that our destination was to be an airfield at Bien Hoa, South Vietnam, arriving about 3:30 in the morning local time. Even before we landed at Wake Island, he had come back over the loudspeaker to inform us that Tan Son Nhut, the final destination, had been changed to Pleiku, about 200 miles north of Saigon. Tan Son Nhut was under a mortar attack.

A few hours after leaving Wake Island, we had another announcement from the cockpit that there was another change of plans; we were now heading once again for Bien Hoa! Pleiku it seemed was now under siege. As we continued our flight, as though we did not already have enough on our minds about what our immediate future had to offer, the flight crew kept us informed, step-by-step, as to the developments on the ground where we intended to land.

We progressed toward Bien Hoa, and, as time passed, it seemed there was increasing enemy activity in progress right about where we had intended to set down. The crew was quite good at keeping our old "pucker factors" right up where they needed to be. At Tan Son Nhut, near Saigon, our newly designated landing site, there seemed to be a rocket or mortar attack in progress, and I think we were all in agreement it would not be in our best interests to land at that particular time and place. That, too, let up and we actually did land there. Well, we were not entirely sure we even wanted to exit the aircraft, but everything turned out fine. I am still not convinced the flight crews don't put you through all that nonsense just for effect, or even for their own entertainment for that fact. I have heard very similar stories from other people, nearly identical stories!

I sometimes think landing us right in the thick of things might have been the very best indoctrination possible for all newly arriving soldiers. However, I really do not believe we could sell the Air Force on that concept. Was the entire scenario a preplanned program for us? Who knows? I do have some suspicions however. Possibly, it was a way to show us the training was over; it was now time for the real thing. If that were the case, it worked quite well. I think the flight was excellent preparation for just about anything that might confront us from the landing site.

I'm really not certain as to whether a flight into Vietnam by day or by night would have been preferable. I arrived in the country during the hours of darkness. Some came in during daylight hours. To see or not to see: that is the question. Do you really want to see what is coming up, or do you want it to be a big surprise? Either way the imagination can go wild. From several thousand feet up some might have seen nothing at all unusual in their approach. Those would either have to presume all this war "stuff" was a bunch of hype, or, of course, they could imagine the very worst happening. In any case, reality was still pretty far off for most new arrivals.

Along with all of the above activities, just to add to the stress level a bit, the normal flight procedures for aircraft landing at airstrips in Vietnam, and I am quite sure it is no different from any other combat zone in today's environment, were a little different than perhaps expected in most non-combat areas. Just before landing, and from several thousand feet elevation, the plane would take an extremely steep dive to the runway, which actually seemed like the aircraft had lost power and was dropping to its final doom! Hey, upon arrival we were all going to die. Why would anyone have wanted to warn us about that part of the flight anyway? It was all part of the excitement of the arrival. "Good training," as we would always say.

I am also sure the flight crew absolutely loved the reactions of all of the unsuspecting troops. How else were they supposed to entertain themselves with all of these back-to-back trips? If they had not been able to add some humor to it all, it could have been very depressing. After all, everyone was aware that many of these troops were never coming back, except maybe in a body bag. Those are the men and women whose success stories ended at that point. For others, and I include myself, their stories had hardly begun.

After having gone through the reception station, the replacement battalion and the appropriate orientation activities for all in-coming troops, my assignment was to an infantry company as the new weapons platoon leader. Probably my first close encounter with the enemy, whom we referred to as Charlie, was after two or three days of being at my unit. (As an aside, many of my readers may not be aware of why we referred to the bad guys as Charlie. The Viet Cong were the local sympathizers with North Vietnam. We abbreviated that name to VC. Using the phonetic alphabet, we have Victor Charlie, which we shortened again to Charlie.) Anyway, I was beginning to get a little crusty, and it was time for a shower. The unit had at our shower point an Australian shower bucket (five-gallon canvass bag with a showerhead) attached to a tree, located near the center of our compound or company perimeter.

I stripped down and wrapped a white towel, one of several I had bought at a military exchange before leaving the States, around my waist, and headed toward the shower point. About half way there, with the towel displayed like a white flag about my loins, shots rang out, popping right over my head. I hit the dirt at nearly the speed of the bullets coming in at me and proceeded to low-crawl back to my tent which had sand bags stacked a couple of feet high around the outside of it. I think I recall arriving at my tent without the white towel. I didn't need it anymore anyway, right? I was certainly not ready to surrender.

I don't recall whether or not I ever continued with my shower mission that day, but I can guarantee my next mission was to invest in some nice olive drab towels which would not set me off as such an enticing target the next time I attempted a shower. I would have to identify that incident as an early lesson learned in quite literally covering my ass, and one for which my Vietnam orientation folks did not adequately prepare me. I think I had a valid complaint, but, to my recollection, I never formalized that complaint. I always accepted responsibility for my own risk-taking, and that was a bit risky, except for the fact that our sniper was not a very good shot. He never hit anyone to my recollection.

That was only one small, early challenge of my tour, and I consider it a minor victory, in that I am still here to relate that humorous story to others. That was just one of many I had to tell by the time I left the country. That incident was also the first time I felt a personal connection when someone decided to line me up in his crosshairs and take a pot shot at me. At the same time, it was not necessary to take it personally since I was not the only target. We were all targets of opportunity. That also was not the last time someone attempted to put me in his crosshairs. It seemed to happen quite frequently actually.

After a little over three months in the northern part of the country, I went south to the 199th Light Infantry Brigade, south of Saigon (now Ho Chi Min City). That move was termed an "infusion program," the intention of which was to balance out the troop levels of units in Vietnam. One of the first of my memorable moments with my new unit I would classify as a lesson in humility. Even though I was perhaps considered a seasoned veteran with three months of combat already behind me, I was still new to this part of the country, and there were a number of things to learn about the area that were considerably different from anywhere else in the country.

Photo 1 - Author moving out from tent to go on patrol - 196th LIB.

Everything south of Saigon is the Mekong Delta. There are certain times of the year, as well as certain times each day, when there is water as far as you can see. All of the rice paddies may be full of water from the rising of the tides, there are more rivers and canals than you can imagine, and it might well be raining at the same time, bringing the water levels even higher. We were wet from the rain, the water through which we were slogging, or from perspiration alone, but we seemed to be wet the vast majority of the time. We could not wear socks or underwear, or we would mold. The rashes that would develop would be too much to endure.

Shortly after arrival to my new infantry company, I received orders for a night ambush. I assumed my position as platoon leader as if I had been with them forever, and, I might add, as if I really knew what I was doing. I honestly felt I had to act that way in order for them to have some element of confidence in their new leader (if you want to consider a second lieutenant a leader). Anyway, I was in charge.

Photo 2 - Overlooking northern terrain and area of operations, monitoring skirmish between Viet Cong and South Korean Ranger unit and napalm strike - 196th LIB.

A short time after departing the company area to our ambush site, we came upon a small canal to cross. We stopped, and all of the men began to break out all their river-crossing gear. My immediate comment was, "What are you doing? This is not a river. It's a little puddle-jumper! We can walk across this thing." One of the men saw me starting toward the canal, raising my rifle over my head, and said, "Sir, I don't think you better try that." I, of course, ignored that silly comment and continued to march, a little on the arrogant side and thinking to myself, "What a bunch of wimps." That attitude did not last long.

I went in knee-deep, waist-deep, chest-deep, and, before I knew it, the water was not only over my head, but also over the top of my raised rifle. My next comment was, "Glub, glub" -- translated, "Oh, shit!" After my men had begun to contain themselves and their laughter, while I was under water, one of my taller

Photo 3 – Mekong Delta at typical low tide.

men came out, grabbed me, and hauled me back to where I could walk back out of the water. Without the slightest hesitation I merely said, "What are you waiting for? Blow up those air mattresses and let's get across this canal." I am very sure I gave most of my men a moment to remember, and I certainly did learn another good lesson of my own.

Before changing subjects and geographical areas, there was one more situation in the delta that merely turned out somewhat embarrassing once again, but really could have been disastrous. It all had to do with the water again and the tidal changes. Yes, I did say tidal changes. The ocean tides control the water levels of the entire Mekong Delta, and the ocean was not in view from where we were, unless we were several thousand feet up in a helicopter. That was something else that someone probably should have warned me about before my first long-range operation.

Photo 4 - Typical river crossing site necessary to negotiate frequently.

It was time again to take my platoon out on a night ambush, but this one was a very long way from our company base camp. I had to travel fifteen or twenty kilometers to get there. I did all my homework. First, I did a map recon and studied the route thoroughly. I then flew the route in a helicopter, map in hand (aerial recon). I identified three minor canals or small river crossings, just as I saw on the map, and no other obstacles. It seemed to be a relatively easy journey to my ambush site, even though it was a long way to walk.

I calculated it would take approximately five and a half hours to get to the vicinity of our ambush site. Leaving a little extra time, I figured if we left by 1:30 in the afternoon (I will use what active Army personnel used

Photo 5 - The Mekong Delta area of operations (AO).

to call National Guard time just to keep it simple), we would be where we needed to be before moving into our designated site just after dark. That would have been about 7:00 P.M. Rather than running into those three expected minor stream crossings, we encountered seven major rivers to cross. I thought to myself, "Where in the hell did all that water come from?"

Yes, indeed, the tide had made a major change since I last observed it from the air. Everything that could have filled up with water did. We did not make it on time to our site. (Duh!) Rather than the projected time of 7:00 P.M., we were still on the move at midnight. It was sometime after midnight we found the spot at which I at least thought we were supposed to be, and set up.

Thank God, we did not have to pull off a real ambush that night. Today I am still not entirely sure we were in the right place. I can hardly express how unnerving it is to be out there walking through the blackness of the

Photo 6 - Flying into Lang Duk.

night, only hoping you are where you are supposed to be. There is one thing of which I was very sure, however, and that is that we were not in friendly territory, and our old friend, Charlie, being on home ground, knew much more about the area than we did, and most of the time knew right where we were. Have I mentioned anything about lessons learned?

In any combat environment, surprises seem to pop up everywhere. It would not matter if it were Vietnam nearly fifty years ago or Afghanistan much more recently. My company was out on a routine sweep one day only to check out an area with suspected enemy activity. As seldom as we found the enemy when we were looking for him, that day we had no problem finding him. We had a suspected NVA company- or battalion-sized element dug in, and we had to flush them out and destroy them. They were in a thick nippa palm grove, and, although we seldom saw them, we were drawing heavy fire from several directions.

We threw everything at them that we had at our disposal. We used our own mortars, called in artillery, and then called upon the Air Force for an air strike. We hit them with napalm and high explosive rounds; so much of it you would not think a rat could have survived it. When it came time to move in on those who might have survived, they shot at us from everywhere. They had apparently dug in so well nothing could have penetrated them. We were finally able to overrun them, most having withdrawn to destinations unknown.

As my platoon progressed through the nippa palm grove, we came under fire from a stay-behind sniper, and we could tell immediately where he was. That was unusual. He was hiding in a bomb crater left by the previous air strike. It was about half full of water, and the NVA soldier kept popping his head up and taking shots at us. One of my young heroes decided on his own to take a giant step forward for himself and his comrades, and he tossed one of his hand grenades into the hole. It seemed like a good, logical thing for him to do, and I would not argue that point most of the time.

On this occasion, however, our adversary was no fool. He kept his head and was somehow able to find that grenade and throw it right back at us! I saw it coming up out of the hole right away and yelled, "Hit the dirt!" No, I did not jump on it. As we flattened out on the ground, it exploded, but miraculously no one was hurt. At that point, I was tired of this guy and had to do something. I had a percussion grenade hanging on my web gear, although I seldom had a use for that type of grenade. It is the type of grenade that does not throw out metal fragments, but rather employs a high explosive impact.

I crawled up close to the hole, and with my men covering me, pulled the pin on my grenade, waited about three seconds and tossed it into the hole. We call that "cooking it off," not a recommended procedure under most conditions. It can be quite dangerous for the thrower since each fuse on a hand grenade is set for four to five seconds of burn after pulling the pin and releasing the handle, just prior to detonation. Relying on that fact can kill you. When you "cook off" a grenade, you just pray you do not have a short fuse. Anyway, after it exploded, I emptied the twenty-round magazine from my CAR-15 into the hole, and we did not hear from that young man again.

Although I may have created the next situation, which resulted in a good-news/bad-news ending, I would not go so far as to say I was entirely at fault; all right, I may admit 90% of the blame. Our company was located in Lang Duk village, probably twenty-five or thirty miles south of Saigon. Two of my men had become very close to two young ladies of the village who happened to be sisters. They were beautiful girls of French and

Vietnamese descent. One day a South Vietnamese National Police jeep with two police officers pulled into the village, and it seemed the first thing they noticed was there were two very attractive, young women standing around within their view.

Photo 7 - Village of Lang Duk shortly after my arrival.

They immediately drove over to the girls and proceeded to arrest them for prostitution. I went over right away to intercede. The officers could speak English quite well, and there was no problem communicating. The first thing I said to them was that I knew the girls and they were perfectly all right, and they were not guilty of prostitution. I never mentioned the fact that, if they wanted to arrest women for prostitution, they just had to go up to Saigon, and they could find them on every street corner. It is funny, however, that the police in general never seemed to bother the real prostitutes for their occupations. In my village, however, it seemed to be different.

I was insistent and they were insistent, and we could not seem to come to terms. The truth of the matter was they wanted the girls for themselves, and that was obvious. I was not going to let it happen. "Push came to shove" and I finally pulled out my .45 cal. automatic,

Photo 8 - Morning after rocket attack – our hooch had been right in front of the bunker.

which I almost never had with me, as I relied on my CAR-15 nearly all the time. Sticking the .45 to the driver's head, I said, "Get the fuck out of here before I blow your head off!" I was very serious; it was not a bluff. Reluctantly, they did leave, but you could tell they were more than just a little irritated. I sometimes reflect upon my reaction under the circumstances, and still know today I did the right thing. I have no idea how I would have gotten away with shooting them had that been necessary, but that was not part of my thinking process at the time. However, there were still repercussions to follow.

The following night I and several other people, to include two other officers, several NCO's and other enlisted men and, I believe, even the two girls previously mentioned, were sitting in a hooch (Vietnamese thatched hut), and we were all socializing and playing

Photo 9 - More destruction in my platoon sector – rocket attack.

cards. None of us expected anything out of the ordinary to happen that night, and, in fact, I did not even have my boots on. I was wearing Vietnamese plastic sandals.

Suddenly there was the loudest explosion any of us had ever encountered. The whole village resounded and shook. We just froze in place, having no idea what just hit us. Just a few seconds later, there was a second identical explosion, and that one had our attention completely. I yelled out for everyone to head for the corner bunker, which was only about twenty feet away. Just as we all scrambled into the bunker, the third round hit, and that was a direct hit on the hooch we had just occupied. Had we delayed another twenty or thirty seconds, we all would have been history.

It occurred to us shortly after the first round hit that we had come under a rocket attack. We could hear them roaring in just before impact. After a few more rounds had come in, it seemed to me the rounds were coming in closer to the bunker each time. I decided that after the next round hit, we would beat feet down the dyke to the next bunker. We did just that and, I think, three more rounds came in, and then they just stopped. Maybe our "friends" just ran out of ammunition. For whatever reason, we were thankful they stopped.

I suppose we were all rather self-centered during that attack, as we were so busy trying to protect ourselves, we were not even aware of what was happening to the regular villagers at the time. The sounds of women and children running around screaming bloody murder, and fire leaping into the night sky a hundred feet or so as their grass huts went up in flames did not escape our attention however. Amazingly, there were no American, and very few civilian casualties.

I took some photographs the next day of the aftermath, and it only occurred to me several years later, after I had seen those slides at least ten or fifteen times, maybe more, that the corner bunker, the first one we had gone into, had taken a direct hit by one of the rockets. There was a huge chunk out of the roof of the bunker right at one of the front corners. The next rocket must have hit that bunker right after we left it to go to the second bunker. That would mean we had been in two locations, the hooch and the first bunker, both of which had taken direct hits right after our having been in them.

Photo 10 - Part of the village closer to the second bunker to which we ran.

After having considered all the facts and evidence, it was relatively easy to conclude someone had indeed known where we were and had directed fire on us, making corrections as we moved. They were following our every move. Those National Police had to have been VC, if not North Vietnamese regulars, and there probably was someone inside the village assisting them as the attack continued.

That was indeed an encounter to remember. Was it a success story or what? It was not enjoyable for those of us who went through it, and much worse for some of the villagers who, unfortunately, lost property and loved ones. I do need to follow all the bad news with some good news. Not one soldier was injured, something for which we could all be thankful. I was perhaps even more thankful than most, considering I was the one person most responsible for the event. I was willing to take the risk, and it did pay off in the long run.

Photo 11 – Impact crater of 122mm rocket. (Small hole to the right is the entry point of the impact.)

If we were to look at the statistics of the Vietnam War, we would find we sent entirely too many people home with injuries from accidents, right along with those who sustained injuries from hostile fire. We did the best we could to preclude accidents from happening, but the hazards of the job made it impossible to stop them all. I emphasized safety continuously, which is not to say all followed the advice. Hey, it was, and still is, difficult for me to follow my own excellent advice.

One of the problems we had was with the safety switch on the M-79 grenade launcher, and we had two of them in every squad. That means I had six to eight grenade launchers in my platoon at all times. The safety switch on that weapon was unreliable. Ensuring the safety switch was engaged did not necessarily mean the weapon would not fire. I insisted that my grenadiers carry that weapon without a round in the chamber or with the breach open, as it was a breach-loaded weapon, just like many shotguns. Well, sometimes we were in areas where it was wise to be ready for action immediately, and it took way too long to load that weapon when someone was shooting at you. There was a need to return fire immediately. So, most were understandably reluctant to follow my rules. I could not enforce such rules when lives were at stake.

Photo 12 - The first bunker in which we took cover (notice sandbags relocated from top of bunker to ground in front – blown off).

As much as I told the members of my platoon I wanted no John Wayne impersonators, I always seemed to have the guy who was toting his M-79 loaded and the breach closed, swinging it back and forth as he walked, and, of course, with his finger on the trigger. On one occasion, one of my fine young soldiers pulled the trigger by accident, the round going straight forward, striking the leg of the man in front of him. Fortunately, the round is designed in such a way that it must travel thirty or forty meters before it detonates. The round did break most of the major bones in the man's leg, which meant he was "dusted off" by the med-evac chopper, and we never saw him again. I was so angry with that grenadier I could have shot him myself. No, it was not really my fault, but I did accept the responsibility. I was the man in charge, per usual.

There was another young man in my own platoon whom I lost due to an "accident," and I am not convinced even today it was actually an accident. We had been out on an operation in the jungle and had hacked our way through thick jungle growth with machetes for a couple of hours. Being more than ready for a break, we stopped for fifteen or twenty minutes. When it was time to hit the "road" again, we got to our feet and gathered up all of our gear. My young friend, to help himself back up into the standing position, grabbed his rifle, left hand at the end of the barrel, index finger over the muzzle of the weapon, right hand grasping the trigger housing, right index finger on the trigger, and proceeded to pull himself up. Need I go further? Why not? Yes, the weapon discharged and the left index finger disappeared into the ether. It was dust-off time again, and that was again one more soldier who would never return to us. That was an easy way out of the field. Though I could be wrong, I feel he probably made a conscious decision to lose a finger rather than taking a chance of losing his life. That was always a choice, but in so doing, the individual would leave his unit one person short. I happen to feel that a person has to be a little nuts to do something like that, as well as terribly disloyal to his fellow soldiers. Fortunately, it was a rare occasion. Those rare occasions, however, are the ones that make me uncomfortable when some voice that all who wore the uniform are heroes. There are some who proved not to be heroes.

Another situation we dealt with from time to time, which I might also classify under accidents, was when we came under "friendly fire." I am sure you have heard plenty of stories of that happening and wondered why or how such things seem to occur so frequently. A great number of my readers, I'm sure, have been through similar experiences. Many of our combat casualties, as I have indicated, were not because of hostile fire. Often the problem exists because of errors made on someone's part, and it could be either a giver or requester of fire support. It can be in the way of artillery support, naval gun support from battleships off shore, Air Force air strikes or Army gunships coming in to offer close air support. It can also be from our own company mortar support or the result of contact between friendly ground troops. One may mistake friendly units for enemy troops and open fire on them. It is all a matter of coordination between the giver and receiver of fire support or coordination between friendly units, and all parties being aware of the location of all friendly units. If the people in support know exactly where you are and where you want their fire directed, then, more than likely, you will get it where you want it. If all of that does not happen, then all parties involved could be in a lot of serious trouble.

Most of the problems I experienced were with our own Army gunships coming to support our operation, and somehow there was a breakdown in communications. One in particular was probably the fault of my company commander, who proved himself in my opinion to be an incompetent field commander. While we were in contact with enemy soldiers in the open, we were seemingly outnumbered and the company commander called for gunship support. It came very shortly, but the pilots were apparently not entirely sure of our location and the enemy location. They mistook our unit for the enemy and came in right on top of us.

We had mini-gun fire peppering our entire area, 3.5-inch rockets exploding all around us, and 40-millimeter grenades going off everywhere. It was quite scary, to say the least, and we always got a good feeling of empathy for our enemy when that happened. Most of us just curled up like turtles under our helmets, as tough as that might be, and made the best of a stressful situation. Our true hero of a commander, however, totally freaked and started running. He stumbled over a rice paddy dyke and dislocated his hip, although, as I just recently discovered, most of the men thought he had been wounded by hostile fire. He was dusted off, nevertheless, and we never saw him again. I am reasonably sure he had given the helicopter pilots an inaccurate location as to exactly where we were and where the enemy was.

There is another occasion where I will blame the Army pilots, because I was the one calling it in. Honestly, this time I really did know where I was. We were in a very hot firefight with NVA regulars, and they had us hopelessly pinned down, such that we could hardly move without being hit. We were in need of help and it was available. I gave my location and the location of our adversaries. The gunships came in and I threw green smoke to let them know my platoon location. I was in direct contact with the pilots and told them where the enemy was in relation to my own position. They were just to the south of us. Sure enough, they came in right through my green smoke and over the top of us and shot us up very effectively.

Those choppers were putting extremely precise fire right where the gunners thought it should be, but they were just a little off. I don't recall anyone taking a hit that day, but those "good guys" certainly were able to get our attention without much effort. Man, I was on my radio, yelling at them to get off my ass, and direct their fire a couple of hundred meters south of where they just put it. On the second attempt, they were much more effective. They took care of business so we could do the same on the ground. Things do happen now and then that do not always turn out the way we plan. We just have to be thankful for the intended help. Our air support was usually fantastic.

There were a few times during my tour in Vietnam that I thought I might still be wearing that white towel wrapped around my waist, without being aware of it. Two of those occasions involved a couple of Viet Cong, or NVAs, carrying rocket-propelled grenade launchers and deciding to zero in on me. Either of those occasions might have been responsible for the initial stages of paranoia setting in. In any case, I was reasonably sure those guys were out to get me, and they were doing a very effective job of it. In reality that was part of the territory that went right along with being in an infantry platoon leader position.

Even back in OCS, the instructors were always trying to scare us by telling us what the life expectancy of a rifle platoon leader was. The figures they gave us were not very encouraging. After all, it did make good sense to our enemy to knock off the leaders first. While I was in Vietnam, I began to believe some of the figures they had given us. At the time, of course, we just shrugged it off as more harassment. The instructors really were trying to get our attention, even though they may have exaggerated a few times. They also had to add before every lecture, "If you are not paying very close attention to what we are presenting here, you will die in Vietnam." After a while, that just became monotonous and irritating, regardless of how close to the truth it may have been.

One occasion where the enemy singled me out, and this incident might again sound familiar if you read my previous book, was when my company was again on a rather lengthy operation in the Mekong Delta, and we had been in contact (engaged with the enemy) most of the day. We broke contact in the afternoon and were ready to think about where to stop for the night. We were in the middle of some very hostile territory with enemy forces all around us, and yet we had no options but to stop for the night.

Someone selected the location for our night position, and I have no idea at what level the decision was made. That choice, however, was absolutely ridiculous. There is no way I would ever have chosen such a location to spend the night. It was right in the middle of a rice paddy, which left us completely open to attack. There were open fields of fire in nearly every direction, which was the good part for us, but the bad part was that we were so vulnerable, being the proverbial "sitting ducks." We were able to procure rolls of concertina wire (wire with razor-sharp edges) to establish a more secure perimeter since we anticipated the probability of big trouble that night. It was very seldom that we were ever able to attain that wire. As it became dark, the weather took a change for the worse. It began to rain and continued throughout the night.

As the night turned into early morning, the most logical time for VC or NVA attacks, sure enough, the inevitable occurred. They planned and executed a massive, early morning attack. The ideal conditions of darkness and bad weather materialized, and they took advantage of it. Through the torrential rain and the darkness, there were sudden bursts of automatic weapons fire, seemingly from everywhere, and explosions outside and within our perimeter, both enemy and friendly. With each flash of an explosion, there were silhouettes of enemy soldiers coming at us. I could not recall ever having seen so many enemy soldiers attacking our position all at the same time. It was indeed overwhelming. Lying in open rice paddies with that flood of rain coming down, we were all in water up to our necks, firing over the mud dykes in front of us, most of the time not even seeing specific targets at which to aim.

In the midst of the fire fight an RPG rocket swished in right between me and my platoon sergeant, Sergeant Joe Terrell, and thumped into the side of the mud dyke about five feet away from both of our heads. There always seems to be good news and bad news. The good news, and I would have to inflate that to wonderful news, is that the round never detonated, and I am, therefore, able to sit here at my computer and write about it. The bad part is the two of us had time to look at the round sticking in the mud, wondering at what moment that delayed fuse might ignite and take both of us with it.

It was fantastic the round did not explode. For several moments, however, we had to think about taking our final breaths, although in reality probably neither of us was even breathing during those rather intense moments. I am reasonably certain I was holding my breath. That was undoubtedly the scariest moment of my life, and Sergeant Terrell seemed to agree when I had a chance to speak with him a few years ago. I am the first to admit to having been scared. Anyone who does not admit to that is either lying or is crazy. My stress level at that point was about as high as it could ever possibly be under any conditions. Although I have never actually feared the thought of death, making the transition from life to death, like being blown up, has never appealed much to me. I would classify that as fear, no doubt.

The next situation involving one of my NVA "buddies" with an RPG launcher was once again in the Mekong Delta. This one begins with an operation initiated by all the activity during the Tet '68 (Chinese New Year) offensive in South Vietnam in the surrounding areas of Saigon. The mission of my unit, the 199th Light Infantry Brigade (LIB), included guarding the southern approaches to Saigon. My platoon was assigned an extremely simple and routine mission to go on a patrol to check out activities in the southern part of the city. We had a very simple mission: to observe what was going on and report what we saw. It was little more than a routine, short recon patrol.

We began our patrol at the southern part of a road leading north into the city. We were to proceed north for a kilometer or so, turn right (east) at a major intersection, continuing for approximately another thousand meters and make another right, heading south, returning to our base of operations. It all sounds simple, right? I always remember the old Jell-O commercial on television that claimed "All that wiggles is not Jell-O." What a wonderful philosophy, which had certainly never occurred to me as a dumb kid. However, later in life I have been able to apply that concept to a tremendous number of situations where things do not always turn out the way you might have imagined.

We headed north from our starting point and found that all along the left flank of our designated route everything seemed quite normal. There were the usual activities among the people; motor vehicles, mopeds, bicycles and pedestrians all seemed to be moving along and milling about with absolutely nothing interfering with what one might expect on a very typical day in Saigon. We reached the intersection where we were to turn right and head east on the north leg of our route. We noticed exactly the same things going on along that segment of the route; again, nothing was out of the ordinary. We did nothing in the way of house-to-house searches; we merely observed of all activities along the route, looking for anything that might seem unusual for that area.

We came to the next intersection where we were to head back to the south and return to our base camp. After a short distance, it occurred to us the situation had changed remarkably and abruptly. Activity in this area was not only abnormal but had ceased entirely. All traffic had disappeared: no vehicles, no people. There was nothing but an eerie silence.

At that point, I instructed all of my squads to proceed much more slowly and cautiously, looking carefully into every house and building along the way. As we proceeded down the street, we noticed a canal on our left flank. A couple of hundred meters or so to the south, on the far side of the canal, was a Vietnamese P.F. (Popular Forces) camp. The popular forces were similar to our state National Guard forces; they were the citizen soldiers. As we continued further, we noticed that ahead of us was a barricade across the road. It was composed of a variety of junk wrapped with barbed wire.

As we proceeded down the road toward the barricade, the PF soldiers, observing our approach, called out to us in broken English from across the canal, "No further, G.I.; bouquet (always pronounced by the Vietnamese, and American troops as "bookoo") V.C." They were giving us a warning that was perfectly clear. There was a large group of enemy soldiers to our front. I had a few options at my disposal, but, silly as it may seem now, I opted for doing things the "right" way. I brought my company commander up on the radio and requested permission to recon by fire. That merely meant I wanted to open up with small arms fire, and see what we might receive in return, thereby identifying enemy targets and taking the offensive.

What was the response to my request? "Negative!" I immediately came back with, "Say again, over."

"Negative on that request. There may be innocent civilians in the area," was his response.

I was dumb-founded. I came back with, "Six (commander's designation or call sign), let me make myself perfectly clear. I have friendlies to my left who have told me very clearly there are Victor Charlies (VC'S or Viet Cong) to my front on the other side of the barrier. Now, once again, request permission to recon by fire! Over."

"Three-six, this is six. I say again, Lieutenant, (a very significant breach in communications security) permission denied! Consider this a direct order. Proceed forward until you make contact. Do you roger that?"

"Affirmative, six, but a couple more requests: Have med-evac on-call, as we will take casualties. Also, request that you, too, be on-call, as I am quite sure we will need assistance. Over."

"Roger that; will be ready to assist. Out."

Well, there I was with a "direct order" to proceed with what I considered a potential suicide mission from a company commander for whom I had little respect (and we were both of equal rank, first lieutenants, he with about three months' time-in-grade on me). I then initiated "my plan." As soon as I had my first three people across the barrier, all hell broke loose with small arms and automatic weapons fire, grenades and RPGs. All three men who had maneuvered across the barrier were wounded and needed immediate extraction and a med-evac.

That med-evac did not exactly happen immediately however. Our enemy had pinned us down with little ability to move without them cutting us to pieces. Somehow, in the midst of all that chaos, we managed to get the wounded to safety and eventually evacuated. At the same time all this was going on, I was finally able to get back to my company commander by radio, to inform him of the situation. He assured me he was on his way with the remainder of the company. I waited for what seemed an eternity while the situation worsened, becoming even more critical.

Although many of the details are hazy, somewhere amid all this chaos, during this rather hellacious firefight, an RPG round quickly caught my eye just before it exploded only three to four feet from me, sending me ten or fifteen feet through the air. After recovering myself, taking an inventory of all of my arms, legs, fingers, etc., and discovering I miraculously did not have a drop of blood flowing from my body, and totally amazed at being unscathed once again, I continued the mission. I quickly thanked the Lord for having my guardian angel(s) looking after me once again, as well as those men who were in very close proximity to me. I often wondered if that legion of angels looking after me was getting extra pay for all the time they spent with me and those close to me. I was prone to being in the wrong places at the wrong times, and it seemed to happen only too regularly.

While all this was going on, and I still had neither seen nor heard from my company commander since he told me he was on his way to assist, I was finally able to bring him back up on the "horn" to find out his status. As one might expect, the main force of the NVA element had pinned him and the rest of the company down on their way to rescue my platoon. My rescuers were in the middle of their own ambush and were now immobile. Needless to say, but of course, I'll say it anyway: I had mixed emotions on that one.

The result was a tank company came to my rescue and leveled that part of the town with their main guns and 50-caliber machine guns. I am not at all certain of it, but we may well have lost a few "innocent" civilians during this cleanup phase. I learned later five or six additional infantry battalions came to join in the "fun" that day.

After my platoon had initiated that whole mess, I had to ask myself why my commander denied my original request. The day turned into a major victory, and, therefore, I never pursued the question. I am also convinced that a little divine intervention played a role in the sequence of events. What could easily have been a disaster turned into something very positive. War is very risky business, even when played according to the "rules."

Photo 13 - Southern Saigon street, similar to that where the above battle took place.

After over nine months of duty in Vietnam, I finally received my opportunity for an R&R to Sydney, Australia, only after a long and costly battle with my battalion commander. It was a wonderful week that truly gave me the rest, as well as the recreation that I needed. Upon my return, I found the unit was right in the middle of what was termed the May Offensive. The NVA had stepped up their activities, such that it was, for our area of operations, even more intense than the Tet Offensive.

After I rejoined my unit, we were in continuous contact with the enemy for at least six days with a few short reprieves. We had very little sleep during that time, and Charlie was wearing us down. At last, our battalion commander, possibly even brigade or higher, gave the order for us to break off and go to a fire support base to sleep it off for the night.

Photo 14 - Some areas of southern Saigon are nearly under water.

We were very relieved to get that news. For our short visit to the fire support base, the unit commander gave us some unoccupied, small bunkers, and cots on which to sleep, which was something of a luxury for us. The bunker my platoon headquarters had was only large enough for two people to occupy. My platoon headquarters consisted of four people. My platoon sergeant, again Sgt. Terrell, and I set up in the bunker, and my radio telephone operator (RTO) and medic had cots just outside the bunker. We settled in about 10:30 that night, more than ready for a good night's sleep. I believe all four of us had already wrapped up in our poncho liners on our cots when our brief rest was abruptly interrupted.

The first explosion rang out before we were even able to drop off to sleep, popping our eyes right open. I immediately called for the men outside to get their asses into the bunker as fast as their feet could carry them. My RTO scrambled into the bunker, but my medic, who had only been in country a few weeks, hesitated too long. The next round that came in was a direct hit on our bunker, and it caught him right in the face and chest, as well as spreading shrapnel all through the bunker and wounding Sgt. Terrell and me.

My medic was one of several fatalities of the night. I found out later over 200 mortar rounds hit us in just a few short minutes. There were several people killed and a much larger number wounded. While I awaited medical attention, I had to watch my medic expire. The chief medic at the battalion aid station told me there was not a thing they could do for him. It seemed to me they could have been doing something, but in reality, it was too late. His chest was bubbling blood, but he was already dead. One of my biggest regrets is that I cannot recall the name of that medic, and I have not found anyone else who can. He was not with us long enough for anyone to have become close to him. That is one of the unfortunate elements of combat.

Finally, I cannot let Vietnam go without sharing one more incident that had nothing to do with my unit or me. After I had been wounded and evacuated, thinking the medical folks would just patch me up and send me back to the field, much to my surprise, they sent me to

Japan without telling me beforehand I was on my way home. While I was at a hospital in Japan, in the bed next to mine, there was a young man who had also been wounded. When I inquired as to what happened to him, he was a little on the hesitant side to share the circumstances of his injury. This is something that just does not happen in real life, but only in humorous fiction stories.

Sometimes truth can be stranger than fiction, and this was one of those times. The man's unit was on an operation of some sort, and they had stopped for a break. Mother nature was screaming at him, and he had no choice but to answer the call. It was time for his daily constitutional. Any sane person would never do that unless a it were a serious emergency. He was very diligent and dug his small slit trench as he had been trained to do. You would never want to leave any of your traces behind, as the enemy would know beyond any doubt you were in his area.

While he was in the process of elimination, sure enough, a sniper had him in his sights, and yes, he did take his shot and caught our friend right in the buttocks. What a way to end a tour of duty! What a horrible thing for a sniper to do! He was playing games. A serious sniper probably would have shot to kill and just shot him in the head, although I am sure the man was quite happy that didn't happen. Can you even imagine that poor man having to tell his children how he was shot in the war? I'm not sure I could even admit to that, even though it would not have been my fault! It was absolutely not his fault. Your heart has to go out to him. War is not just a risky business; it can also be very unfair. The bad guys do not always play by the rules.

Chapter 5 – End of Active Duty

After my tour in Vietnam, I spent some time assigned to the US Army Hospital at Fort MacArthur, California. There was never anything seriously wrong with me, and I was ambulatory all the time I was on convalescent leave. I was having a great time, going off to the beach every day and just generally enjoying life. Maybe someone thought I deserved it. I don't know. What I did know at the time was that, as nice as it might have been, I had had enough of it after a couple of months.

I finally cornered an officer in the admin branch and asked him if they had any plans to give me a job or reassign me somewhere where I could go back to work. He then asked me that killer question, "Where do you want to go?" No one, to my recollection, had ever asked me that question all the time I had been in the Army. I had filled out "dream sheets" before, but it was not as though anyone ever paid any attention to them. The Army always made a steady habit of sending me in the opposite direction of my desires. That is not a complaint, but rather an observation.

I thought about the question for a few moments and answered, "Well, how about my old "home away from home," Fort Benning, or maybe somewhere on the west coast, like Fort Ord, California or Fort Lewis,

Washington? The officer nodded and walked away, and I heard nothing for a couple of weeks. Then someone delivered an envelope to me, containing a set of reassignment orders to Headquarters, Sixth US Army, Presidio of San Francisco, California. Specifically my position was to be an action officer in the DCSOPS (Deputy Chief of Staff for Operations and Training). I could not believe my eyes. I did not even know there were any Army units in San Francisco. That was much more than I could ever have wished.

I have to admit, for a while I really did enjoy that job, since it was such a contrast from the combat environment of Vietnam. After a few months of that desk job, however, things became monotonous. I was not exactly comfortable at a desk, as I was an infantry officer, and that staff position is not what I was trained to do or even what I enjoyed. One day I was sitting in my swivel chair, feet up, drinking coffee, possibly even eating a donut, and I said loudly enough for everyone to hear, "I'd give my right arm for the opportunity to go to Airborne and Ranger School tomorrow. I'm getting a rash on my butt from sitting at this desk too long."

One of the majors with whom I worked had been one of my company commanders in Vietnam for a few months, and we were quite good friends. It was amazing we had ended up together again so soon. He overheard my comment as he was walking through the office, and he disappeared for about ten minutes. He had gone upstairs to the school's branch, and, when he returned, he tossed a couple of sheets of paper on my desk and said, "Here are your class dates, John." Incredulously I asked, "What? Are you kidding me?" Once again, I could hardly believe my eyes. There they were: my class dates for Airborne and Ranger School. I had tried so hard to get those schools out of OCS, but there was no way. Now, ten minutes after I had merely made a comment, mostly in jest, here I was, going away for three months for the schools I had always desperately wanted. May wonders never cease!

The first two weeks of airborne training were pretty much a "piece of cake." The first week was mainly running and continuous exercise. The second week was tower week where we jumped from the forty-foot towers and then the last day of that week from the 200-foot tower. That was great, but not long after my class went through, the school shut the 200-foot tower down forever. There must have been too many accidents. I am very thankful I had a chance to make that jump. The third week was when all the real fun began. That was "jump week" where we actually jumped out of an aircraft from twelve hundred feet. It all sounds cool, and it really is, until things begin to go wrong. Hey, with me who would expect anything else?

There were five jumps that week, and I don't recall which one it was, but on one of them we had some very significant winds. The Air Force pilots were trying to decide whether to drop us or return us to base. It was toward the end of the day, and I am sure they were getting hungry and a little anxious to get home to family and a good meal. The winds kept gusting and then dying down. At last, the pilots grew tired of carrying us around. Rather than taking us back, they decided just to drop us and hope for the best, and, yes, they did have to have approval from our Army jump master who was always along for the ride. I really shouldn't blame the Air Force a hundred percent all the time.

All went well for a little while. We had an excellent drop, my chute deployed beautifully, and my descent was wonderful as usual. It did seem that I was moving horizontally a bit faster than usual, but, other than that, all was going smoothly. However, as I neared the ground, things began to happen very quickly, and I was slipping through the air at a tremendous speed. The wind was now at about thirty-five to forty miles per hour. My body was oscillating wildly back and forth under my canopy. When I was only a few feet from the ground, my body was moving right with the wind, which increased my velocity to probably forty-five to fifty miles per hour. It was like falling off the back of a truck on a California interstate. My classic five-point PLF (parachute landing fall) was probably a twenty-five pointer as I tumbled across the ground head over heels, slowing down very little as I continued.

When I finally came to what was a near stop, the wind grabbed my chute again and off I went across the drop zone. I was going headfirst as if dragged by a ski boat. The parachutes did have quick-release mechanisms, but

I could not get mine to work. I was not exactly a seasoned jumper. As I sailed across the drop zone face-first, I could envision a huge tree stump crushing into my chest. Finally, I was able to deploy the quick-release and my chute collapsed. I was a mess, beat up and aching all over, but I was not through yet. I still had to police up the chute and double-time off the zone, as we had two drops to make that day; so, that meant, move out, get another chute and be ready to jump again. Hooah!

The jumping was not quite over for me after airborne training. For those who were airborne qualified, Ranger School would be providing a few jumps, and most who attended Ranger School had already been through jump school. As I have mentioned, Ranger School provided some memorable moments, to be sure. It is by far the toughest school the Army has to offer with one possible exception. There is a commando force (Delta Force), about which the Army has little to disclose, and that would be one step beyond the Rangers, but it also would not be prudent to discuss that subject here, nor am I qualified to do so. They are all special operations people.

Because I am still on the topic of jumping out of aircraft, I cannot move away from that subject without covering my most notorious jump, and that did happen during my Ranger training. Although during Ranger training we did try to incorporate our scheduled jumps with an actual training operation, it did not always work out that way. One of the jumps was not much more than a routine "Hollywood" jump. The C-130 Air Force cargo plane was taking us to the designated drop zone and everything was progressing nicely. Closing on the drop zone, the green light came on, which meant we were to stand up, hook up our static lines and be ready to exit the aircraft. The jumpmaster began tapping each jumper on the shoulder with an audible "Go!" Each jumper moved to the ramp to step out into the "wild blue yonder."

All chutes should deploy at about four to four and a half seconds, and each man counts as he exits the aircraft. "One thousand, two thousand, three thousand, four thousand," and with any luck at all, you see and feel that open canopy at just about that moment. If your count goes much farther than that, you are probably in some significant trouble. Well, yes, I did feel that wonderful tug of my canopy opening, and there I was, hanging in a slow, easy descent.

All was quiet and peaceful, and absolutely fantastic. There is really nothing in the world more peaceful than that slow meandering descent down through the clouds or clear blue sky with an almost silent whisper of a breeze blowing past your ears. It was time, however, to come out of that little "twilight zone" feeling and back to the reality of the moment. I began to look around in order to get my bearings and figure out where I might be landing. I looked to the front and saw nothing but trees. I looked to the left and then to the right. I grabbed my risers (parachute straps) to twist around in order to see the drop zone behind me. Unfortunately, it was not there either. Now, the drop zone is two miles wide and three miles long. We dropped from twelve hundred feet. Is there any reason why we should not see a drop zone? The answer would be no, if there were one to see. There was definitely a problem. There was no drop zone on which to land, and that is not a pretty picture.

There I was, dropping quickly, and not entirely sure of what direction to head with my semi-steerable parachute. I searched and searched on my way down, not finding so much as a few square feet of clearing; nothing. It was pine needle to pine needle; trees as far as I could see. All I could do was say a quick prayer, which went something like, "All right, Lord, it's just You and me all the way! Ready or not, if You will it, here I come!" After a loud crashing through the upper branches of the trees through which I had fallen, I blacked out for just a few seconds. I opened my eyes to see blue sky and the tops of a few trees. My body could not seem to move a muscle. I actually could not feel anything for a while. Was this death? Nah, probably not.

I was wondering why I could not seem to move when it occurred to me that my risers had bound me to the tree branches. My arms and my legs were tight to the tree, rendering me immobile. As I believe I stated in my first book, I felt like one of the thieves crucified with Jesus, secured at every point. I struggled for five or ten minutes just to begin freeing myself. After another ten or fifteen minutes I had myself nearly free, having actually cut some of the lines that had been holding me. I also cut a few others, which may have helped in lowering myself from that tree. On the other hand, I was a hundred or more feet in the air. These were giant trees!

About the time I was thinking seriously about climbing down from the tree, I heard the sounds of helicopter blades approaching. I looked up to see a huge CH-47 Chinook helicopter coming in to take a closer look at who might still be hanging in the trees. The Air Force and the Army knew what had happened, and they were out there on the scene already looking for us. They had landed fifteen of us in the trees that day. I was one of the more fortunate, since I was not seriously injured. There were a few broken bones among the others. While that Chinook descended upon me, the downward blast from the two big rotors on that bird grabbed the tree I was in and nearly shook me loose from it. I had made it that far, and the rescuers were going to finish me off. Now that would have been very embarrassing for me as well as my rescuers. I would never have lived it down had they killed me at that point. Here again, we had a potential disaster that turned into a successful jump, another one from which I walked away. "I love it when a plan comes together," were the memorable words of Colonel John "Hannibal" Smith, played by George Peppard in the TV series "The A-Team."

After Ranger School, I returned to San Francisco to complete that tour of duty, which was to last a total of about a year and a half. I knew with certainty I would have another tactical assignment after spending time in such a plush environment. Earlier I had put in for the Republic of Korea, as I had no strong desire to return to Vietnam, and that would otherwise have been my next destination. I knew Korea was not going to be another San Francisco, but then that was not in any way what I wanted. I was an infantry officer, and I had been away from my occupational specialty long enough. I wanted to command an infantry company. I did receive an assignment to Korea. Upon arrival in that country, my assignment was to the Second Infantry Division, located far to the north of the capital city of Soule, and just south of the Imjin River.

There were no infantry company command slots open when I arrived, and I became the Division Psychological Operations (Psyops) Officer. In many ways, it was a very interesting job, but was not what I had in mind. It was a challenge trying to think up mind games for the North Koreans, an attempt to change their mindsets and attitudes to be more in line with the democracy to the south. It never has worked of course, but it was fun trying. The idea was to come up with effective leaflets to drop, in order to get them to think about defecting or at least sympathizing with the south. It was generally playing mind games with our potential enemy. The work, interesting as it might have been, did not keep me occupied enough, and my very strong desire continued, which was to have an infantry company of my own.

As time went on, and it did not seem like anyone was listening to my pleas, I became somewhat disheartened. I not only wanted, but also needed command time. An infantry captain never having had command time could not even hope to see a promotion to major. It is part of the career development program and is an absolute necessity. I continued to give my superiors a tough time about my needs and desires, and I think they were receiving a different message than I had intended. I think they began to believe I disliked my job, rather than just wanting a command slot.

I may have been somewhat overly verbal about the whole thing, and perhaps somewhat lacking in the area of tact, which has never been my strongest suit. After a few weeks of that job, my voice was finally heard, but not before my coming very close to receiving a negative OER (officer efficiency report), which would never be good for career development. More than one or two of those can end a career in a heartbeat. My superiors finally gave me my infantry company, and that was the beginning of a great year for me. It was another near failure that turned to success.

I had some very nice experiences during that year of command, and it was exactly what I needed for my own personal growth. I commanded a company that was part of a rotational battalion. We would spend three months up in the DMZ (demilitarized zone), manning guard posts between North and South Korea, and then rotate with another battalion and go south of the Imjin River for three months of training. That continued for the year of my command. It was extremely interesting work, and I enjoyed it very much, including the mandatory training in the south.

I think it was the variety of work with my infantry company that I enjoyed more than any part of that thirteen-month tour. We had great areas for training, as well as actual tactical operations within the DMZ, much of which was spent manning the guard posts far enough inside the zone to see the North Korean guard posts. We could look at them with our binoculars watching us with their binoculars. It was fascinating. To my knowledge, no American forces ever did any active operations within the DMZ during my thirteen months, although my knowledge base might not have been all that extensive. The North Koreans, however, would incorporate within their own training operations, sapper squads that would infiltrate by night within rock-throwing distance of our guard posts, and actually throw rocks at our positions, which, of course, really spooked our guys every time that happened.

When the North Koreans pulled stunts like that, we had no authority to do a thing about it. We were prohibited from shooting at them unless they first shot at us, which never happened in my area while I was there. We could never do the same things to them as they did to us, or that would cause an international incident. It is a little funny how the North Koreans were never particularly concerned about protocol or breaking a few rules. The whole situation was not exactly one of equality. Our rules and their rules were not always quite the same. That was all part of the game, as well as our big challenge while serving in Korea.

Being something of an old rule breaker at heart, I did attempt and get away with a few things in Korea that were not quite "kosher." One of them, which was not my idea, was when the battalion commander gathered up most of the officers of the battalion and we all went pheasant hunting up in the DMZ. That was unequivocally unauthorized, and that was also why the hunting was so great. There were no hunters allowed in that area. We flushed out fifty or sixty pheasant at a time. You could fire a shotgun without even aiming and bring down one or more pheasant. It was great fun that day and we had our Korean chefs make us a beautiful pheasant dinner from the day's successful hunt. Gee, what more could you ask for from a hardship tour?

Another slightly unauthorized thing I used to do was taking photographs where no one is supposed to have a camera. I went out to the guard posts regularly, checking on my men. No one is, under any circumstances, authorized to take photographs within the DMZ without authorization. Everything is classified. Well, I had my Nikon camera with a 200 mm telephoto lens, and I just could not help myself sometimes. I suppose I could have been in a heap of trouble for that, but the temptation was just too much for me. I would be watching those North Koreans watching us, and I just had to have a picture of that. I'm quite sure they had plenty of pictures of us. I also wanted pictures of our own guard posts covered with snow in the winter months. Some of those are beautiful shots.

Photo 15 - DMZ guard post in the winter.

Probably the least pleasant part of that Korean tour was toward the very end of it, when our unit received deactivation orders. The US was downsizing our troop strength in Korea, and my battalion was on the hit list. That was a complicated process, and all commanders were responsible for accounting for all of the property in the battalion in order to turn it in. That was quite an undertaking. Many years had passed since there had been an extremely detailed accountability taken by that battalion. I even found that my supply sergeant, who had gone home a few weeks before, had sold about $700.00 worth of blankets down in the local village and pocketed the cash.

I thought I was in serious trouble until I found out how bad off the other companies in the battalion were, particularly our Headquarters Company. All of the company commanders were "sweating blood," thinking that our losses would come out of our paychecks. When it was all over, the result was we were all exonerated from our liability, which was a tremendous relief. We all

Photo 16 - It did get a little chilly out on the guard posts.

ended up going home free and clear. It was a narrow escape, but a victory nevertheless. That was pretty much the end of my active duty with the US Army. I then headed back to the States and a wedding to begin my transition to a new life within the civilian community.

Referring just for a moment back to the Vietnam War, the perspectives on that war can vary as widely as the perspectives of all who observed and/or evaluated them. Some say we lost the war, even though we won nearly every major battle. The North Vietnamese can probably say in a similar way, even though they lost most of their major and minor battles, they still won the war. I honestly feel there were no winners or losers. The point here is history shows us wars can be won after many battles have been lost, and sometimes that is just a matter of perception. The same is true about life. Success can often be the result of many failures or near failures.

Photo 17 - Border road on the southern side of DMZ; pretty nasty in the winter.

In the case of my own life, I began having academic problems way back in the very beginnings of elementary school. I caught on well when it came to concepts, but my reading skills fell way behind. At the end of my second grade, I was having such difficulties with reading that my mother recommended the school hold me back for a second run at second grade. It really felt at the time I had met with failure. What was the result? I became an English teacher. Failure? I don't think so. It only proves again the old Jell-O commercial philosophy. Things are not always what they seem to be.

The early years of college were not much better for me. I finished high school fairly well with a high 'B' average, but, when I got to college, I struggled much more than I ever thought I would. I was on academic probation for nearly all of my first two and a half years. I felt like I was failing miserably. In the Army, I came close to not making it through OCS. In Ranger School, I did not receive the distinguished Ranger tab. I even had a very tough time mastering knot tying.

After ten years holding the rank of captain, I was denied promotion to major, the Army stating I was not academically qualified, which was not true. I later had to prove it. Just before being retired, the Army erroneously discharged me, rather than retiring me. That took a while to straighten out. Ah, yes, the challenges of life never cease. They just make life more interesting. There is always something more for which to strive. It gives life much more purpose. With the right attitude, it can even be fun.

As my active Army career approached a total of three years, I had some doubts about whether or not I really wanted to remain on active duty for twenty or thirty years, considering how many obstacles there had been for me up to that point in time. There was unending pressure from superiors, which I was not entirely convinced I needed for the rest of a lengthy military career. Therefore, rather than applying for a regular commission (I received a reserve commission from OCS), I applied for a two-year extension to my reserve commission, which would give me some additional time to think about it before committing myself. For one who was considering the military as a full-time career, I might have researched the possibilities a little further before making that decision.

By the time my two-year extension was approaching an end, the Army, as well as all other branches of the military, had begun to cut back its force structure. The RIF (reduction in force) had begun, and I became one of the early statistics. I applied for voluntary indefinite status, which would mean I had no specific date for discharge. I could remain on active duty as long as I desired. That did not work. My application was turned down, in addition to my application for a regular Army commission, and I was to be discharged at the end of my two-year extension. I was, of course, also in Korea and engaged to be married at the end of that tour of duty. That decision by the US Army for my release took me a bit by surprise. I had some reevaluating to do. In retrospect, nothing better could have happened to me, but it would have been very tough to convince me of how wonderful it was at the time.

Chapter 6 – Formal Education to Teaching Career

In December of 1970, I was to return to the US from South Korea only to receive a discharge and transfer to inactive reserve status. In the interim, however, also on the schedule was a military wedding at the Presidio of San Francisco. My fiancé and I had made all of the arrangements and scheduled all of the dates for the activities surrounding the wedding, and those dates were all after my scheduled discharge. Because the Army could not have anything to do with my wedding ceremony after my discharge from active duty, that was not going to work. I had to request a two-week extension on my discharge. Of course, per usual, the Army had to hassle me about it. Finally, I had that approved and was able to go on with the wedding, which ended up being a big mistake anyway, but the wedding ceremony itself turned out very nice, and life in general improved remarkably after that marriage ended. Life in general is the part that I consider the success after a failure at marriage. I will hit you with the details of that a little later.

In conjunction with that rather extensive reevaluation of my career plan was an equally extensive plan for the rest of my life, as well as that of my new wife, Esther. I was fresh out of the Army, unemployed, not having finished a four-year college curriculum, and newly married, with obvious responsibilities in front of me. Fortunately, Esther had her degree and was a practicing medical technologist in San Francisco when I met her. Her family lived in Tucson, Arizona, and she had graduated from the University of Arizona. I needed to finish a program for a bachelor's degree, and, after investigating that school and finding they had a German program, which was my interest, as well as the fact that Esther's family lived in Tucson, the two of us agreed I should enroll at the U of A. I majored in German and minored in English, and I enrolled in the School of Education in order to teach at secondary level.

Esther, having established herself firmly in San Francisco, had no problem getting a job at the University of Arizona Hospital. We moved into a nice apartment near the university and were quite happy there for the first year or so. I also became much closer to her family over that time. I was actually the second "gringo" in the family, as her aunt had married out of the Hispanic domain. He was for a while the "token white guy," but I helped him out of that category. We liked each other very much, and the family had accepted both of us. Her brother had just finished high school, and the two of us were attending the university together. I was just a little envious and a bit resentful of the fact he was so ridiculously bright that he never had to put any effort into receiving straight A's in all of his subjects, and he was in the School of Architecture. I never saw him crack a book all the time I knew him. I had to work my tail off to get my B's. Life was still not fair.

Esther had been a member of a sorority on campus when she had attended the university. She contacted them while we were there, and we found they were looking for a house director at the time. They invited the two of us to become house parents for the sorority. We would have free housing and meals. How could we turn down an offer like that? With no rent and no food expenses to speak of, it could not have worked out better for us. Of course, it was a terrible inconvenience for me, being in a house with fifty or so young college girls. Somehow I made it and without having to whine or complain a great deal to my wife about all the horrible disruptions. We remained there until I graduated, and even a year or so after that for postgraduate work. After two or three years of that sorority experience, I had frequent memory losses, and I have lost track of time. Was that some sort of PTSD? All right, I'm lying again.

Very shortly after arriving in Tucson, I made connections with the US Army Reserve Center in town, as I was interested in furthering my military, as well as my college, education. I needed to take the infantry officer advanced course, a requirement for all company-grade infantry officers. Shortly after beginning the course, someone associated with the school mentioned to me they were looking for someone to take over the Tucson satellite branch of the NCO Academy.

The headquarters for the school was in Phoenix. I expressed a desire for the job and got it. I remained at the school in that capacity all the time I stayed in Tucson. With the coursework I was taking, as well as the drills I was putting in, teaching the NCO Academy students, I was able to generate additional income. With Esther's income, which was quite good, my GI Bill benefits, and my reserve pay, we were not the stereotypical starving students. If we were low on cash assets, it was because we spent too much money, and we were certainly guilty of that.

While attending school in Tucson, I worked very hard to attain an acceptable grade point average, but it's not as though I were an academic superstar. I did much better than I had several years before at San Diego State College, but I still struggled, even in my German major. Nothing ever came easy. Then again, how would that have been any fun if all the challenges were taken away?

I was once cornered by one of my German professors, and he looked me straight in the eye and said in his very broken English, "John, do both of us a big favor, and never become a German teacher." Ouch! That smarted. I am not sure to this day whether he was trying genuinely to discourage me or to encourage me to do better. In any case, he put a challenge before me, and there was no way in hell that I would not become a German teacher after such a comment. I also recall he was the one who wrote the comment on one of my papers, in an attempt to correct my English, "Split never the infinitive." I will always remember that comment because it really hit my funny bone with the irony behind it. I think, because of that comment, however, I very seldom split infinitives.

Although I never got to the point where I considered myself one hundred percent fluent in the language, I think I was a very effective German teacher. One person seemed to consider me a failure, but I managed to turn it into a success. The high school teaching position lasted for twenty years before I decided to quit, and that was due to a lack of support on the part of the administration of that school. That is another long story.

After nearly four years in Arizona, Esther and I decided to move back to California to seek work. She landed a job right away in Escondido, California, just north of San Diego, and that is where we settled. I had applications out all over the San Diego area, and one day someone from a brand new school, opening in Del Mar, gave me a call. We met very informally at a Big Boy restaurant in Encinitas, and in about a half hour, I had a job. Ironically, they thought I was someone else when they called me, but by then it was too late to change. There were then over three thousand applications for teaching positions on file in that district alone. That is one reason I was amazed anyone had even called me. I'm not sure I was working alone to find that position. It seemed to be more than just a coincidence that I nailed that job so easily. Who am I to question something as amazing as that? I am a strong believer in divine intervention.

That high school teaching position was amazing in many ways. It was often a difficult struggle, as well as enlightening and a further development of my own skills as a teacher. It helped me tremendously in my own development as a writer. In the early part of my teaching career, I was undoubtedly weak in my classroom management skills, and my school administrators often interpreted my general demeanor as my having a lack of control over my students, which may now and then have had some elements of truth, but I felt that was seldom the case.

I was never what one would call a staunch disciplinarian with my students, but I did toughen up as time went on. I allowed my students to communicate orally in class, as long as they were working hard on projects. I was both a German teacher and an English teacher, and both classes could get a little noisy at times. It was oral communication. Some viewed it as out of order. I did well with it, and most of my students learned well with it. That was the most important result, and that was what mattered to me. I have also been very strong in the art of denial. I would never admit to ever having any weaknesses in my teaching skills. Don't take that comment too seriously.

Torrey Pines High School was a very interesting environment. Located in Del Mar, California, we had students from Rancho Santa Fe, as well as several other communities, but the Rancho Santa Fe families lived in multi-million dollar homes. Many worked in Hollywood in the entertainment industry. Some were very well known actors and producers. Some were prominent corporate lawyers, wealthy entrepreneurs and professional athletes. The barns in which they kept their horses were nicer than the home in which I lived. Those dwellings may not have smelled nicer than my home, but they did look nicer from the outside.

The student parking lot at that school made the faculty parking lot look like a junk yard. Many of the students had their parents' hand-me-down Mercedes, Porsches, Jaguars and Corvettes. I always will remember the young lady who approached me one day, begging and pleading with me to give her an "A" in her English class. I asked her why she thought she deserved such a grade. Her response was, "Oh, Mr. McClarren, I just have to have that 'A' or I won't get a new Porsche for my sixteenth birthday." I simply came back with, "Oh, my gosh, really? Well, sweetie, I'm thinking that you just might have to wait till your seventeenth birthday, because you are a long way off from an 'A' this semester." She did have a tough time dealing with that one.

While I was destroying a young life with that devastating news, I'm sure I must have been thinking about that old Chevy station wagon that Deb and I had been driving for a while, the engine of which had recently caught fire and burned up, just short of totaling the whole car. You can imagine how terrible I felt about the crisis in which my student found herself. It was heart wrenching. I certainly hope I am not sounding sarcastic in any way. Perish the thought.

I began my teaching career in 1974, which did not put the Vietnam War that far removed in time from my students. In fact, the war was just ending at that time. Many of their fathers and other close relatives had fought in that war. It was much closer to them in time than World War II had been for me when I was in high school, and I was always very interested in the history of that war. My students were, in the same way, interested in Vietnam. I had about a hundred slides from the war, a slide show of which I turned into an annual event.

I showed the slides to all of my students, talked about my experiences, and I tried to dispel many of the nasty rumors that were still around, particularly with regard to most of the Vietnam returnees being crazy or druggies. Many believed the majority of soldiers over there had been into drugs and consequently were all potheads or mentally ill when they returned. Debbie, my present wife, even thought the same way when we first met. It took a little while to convince her otherwise, and, of course, that I was crazy long before going to Vietnam; so, I could not blame that part on my war experiences. My students knew me pretty well by the end of each year and did show a good deal of respect toward me. That, too, helped me in my teaching effectiveness.

As seriously as I took my job, I also had to have fun with it. My philosophy is that, if you cannot enjoy and have fun with your chosen profession, then you have chosen the wrong profession. There was little I hated more than student vandalism during my teaching career. However, I did encounter an incident involving student vandalism I was not able to take as seriously as I probably should have.

One weekend night several students assembled on campus and decided to spray-paint several messages on the sides of our school buildings, mostly our portable classrooms. I don't recall exactly what they were trying to protest at the time, but I do distinctly recall one building, which had a message that did not at all pertain to the protest at hand. It read, "McClarren smokes Agent Orange." All right, I certainly agree, that is vandalism, one thing we should never condone. On the other hand, it did show a great deal of humor and it was very creative in nature. Hey, I had to appreciate that aspect of it, and I have to admit that I got a good laugh out of it. The students neither broke anything, nor did any permanent damage. However, they did have a little weekend work detail to follow, and that was painting over what they had done.

A few years into my high school teaching, and close to seven years into my first marriage, Esther and I came to a point at which we had to depart from one another. We were both just too unhappy in our relationship to create an enjoyable life. Fortunately, we had no children together, and it made the separation that much easier.

Esther had been offered a great position in San Francisco, and I told her to take it. She presumed by that I was agreeable to making the move with her, but that was not the case, nor the intent of my suggestion. I told her to make the move, and I would help her with it. If we decided later we missed one another, then we could make further plans. That never happened and we turned it into a divorce. That seemed like a failure at marriage, but it turned out to be one of the greatest things that could ever have happened, at least for me. It was less than a year later I met Debbie, my present wife of thirty-four years. At this point, I'm thinking we just might make it all the way.

Chapter 7 – Leave of Absence and Travel

To add to my active duty military life, I had an opportunity between my two marriages to see much of the world I had not yet seen. Esther and I had acquired a house and some additional property, both of which had inflated remarkably in value, and, when we went our separate ways, we sold both the house and the property and split the profits. Rather than reinvesting those profits, which would have made good, logical economic sense, I made my own logic, which was to help my psychological state of mind. I was really coming close to "burn-out" in my teaching after the first four years, and there was the fact that after four years of teaching the German language, I had never set foot in Germany. That did not seem right to me. With the money I had from the house and property sales, I could take a year leave of absence from teaching, and use some of that money for travel expenses. I set that plan in place and followed through with it. I looked forward to a great year with no pressures whatsoever.

I submitted an application for my leave of absence, the reason being travel critical to my German teaching, had it approved, finished off the academic year, and I was free to go. My first destination was off to Pensacola, Florida to visit my aunt and uncle and their English friend, Dorothy, who had been with them for years, as almost an adopted daughter. When she heard my next destination was Europe, she told me she intended to go home (England) for Christmas, and invited me to join her and her family for Christmas. It was an offer I could hardly refuse. I accepted and I then had a Christmas plan. I had not even thought about how I might spend Christmas before that invitation.

An additional plan I had was to fly directly to Gothenburg, Sweden to pick up a new Volvo station wagon, which was my other big dream at the time. Fortunately for me, although it really seemed unfortunate at the time, the deal fell through with my credit union at home in California. I only received word a few days before my scheduled flight from England to Sweden. I came very close to going to Sweden to find I did not have a car waiting for me. I would have been more than just a little upset had I proceeded with that plan, although I might well have altered my travel plans to see some of the Scandinavian countries.

I was financially prepared to travel Europe, but there were a few things I had not planned well. I was capable of putting a down payment on a new car, and to make payments thereafter. However, I had not considered the price of gasoline in Europe being twice that in the US. I had also not carefully considered the complications and the cost of having the car sent to the US when it was time for me to come home. I would have been in debt up to my ears had the car deal have gone through. It definitely would not have been cheaper to buy a European car in Europe than to have bought it right

Leave of Absence and Travel | 157

here in the US. The plan did come together, just not as expected. The only major obstacle was the amount of luggage I was carrying to travel. I planned to have a car, but the reality was I would be on foot. I was an old army infantryman; I presumed I could handle it without too much whining. On the other hand, we old grunts (infantry soldiers) are notorious whiners.

Although I could not coordinate my itinerary to coincide with Dorothy's, we still made it to England, she ahead of me by a few days. When I arrived at her parents' house in Hillingdon, Middlesex, she was also there to greet me. We had a very nice time over the Christmas holidays, and her family was wonderful and showed me a remarkable amount of hospitality. Dorothy's brother, Peter, and I became close friends while I was there, and I went off to stay with him and his roommates for a few weeks. They lived in a town, maybe twenty or twenty-five miles from London, by the name of Church Crookham in Aldershot, which is also a military town, as it has one of the largest British Army training centers in the country.

Staying with those guys was very enjoyable, and I really had an interesting introduction to the country. Their house was an absolute mess, however. They were three single, young men living together, and none of them had the inclination to clean anything. I suppose that was one reason for my being there. I did quite a bit of cleanup work for them. I had more time on my hands than anyone else, and I really didn't mind doing it.

In the six weeks or so I was in England it took me a good three weeks to get to a rudimentary understanding of what anyone was saying to me. I believe it was Winston Churchill who said that England and America are two countries divided by a common language. I found that to be a very accurate statement. Americans have been accused of mutilating the Queen's English for years, but I have never heard as much of an abomination of the language as right there in their own country. I once was interested in teaching English in Germany, but was informed they will only hire British teachers to teach English, as Americans do not use proper English. Rubbish, I say. That's just plain poppycock. It's a total misconception by the entire world. Any arguments? I didn't think so. Moving right along.

During my stay in England there are things I would have wanted to see, but was unable to. I did make the most of the time I had, however. I saw nearly all of London, including Westminster Abby and Big Ben, The Tower Bridge and all of the Crown Jewels, St Paul's Cathedral, Madame Trousseau's Wax Museum, and Twenty-One, Downing Street, where the Prime Minister lives. I also crossed the Thames to the Old Globe Theater, and, of course, on to Windsor Castle, where Henry XIII and all his wives once lived (and died). One day a friend of Peter volunteered to take me over to the Salisbury Plains to see the famous Stonehenge, about which I had been studying so much. That was fantastic. I loved it. It was before they cordoned it off to the public; so, I was able to walk around and look very closely at all of the huge monoliths.

Knowing I was going to leave England and head for Germany, Peter decided he would join me in some of my travels. He wasn't making a great deal of money at his job, and he asked me if I could hang about for an extra couple of weeks so he could make a little more money with which to travel, as well as eat. I figured there was still a good deal of England, which I had not yet experienced. Why not? I was not on any strict schedule. It really made no difference to me what I was doing, where I was going or when I might do it. It was a great feeling to be free to do anything I wanted. I would love to have been able to do that forever, but then that would not be a real life.

Peter and I, often with his friends, did quite a bit together. They had their local pub we frequented in the evenings. We shot pool, socialized and drank a fair quantity of stout, ales, bitters, lagers and other brews. There was one evening during which they caught me off guard. Fortunately, it was a Friday night when my new "friends" introduced me to real ale. I was just short of being adequately prepared for that one. I hardly ever drank beer back home; I just never cared much for it. While in England, I definitely acquired a taste for the local brews. After about three real ales, I had my arms wrapped around a large pillar in the middle of the pub. I saw it as my responsibility to hold up the pub, since I was sure it would not have held together without me gripping it throughout the night. The lager and Guinness I had before the real ales may have had something to do with the final result. I can't be sure.

One might think I would have had a terrible morning upon waking up the next day; however, lo and behold, and much to the disappointment of all me mates, I woke up feeling great. I was ready to move out smartly to the Stonehenge. I did not have the slightest headache or upset stomach (at least to which I would ever have admitted). I was in great condition and ready to rock and roll. That would never have happened at home in the US. Too much to drink always meant automatic hangover. Maybe the European beers are better quality. I have no idea, but I am happy I don't do well with drinking here. That would not be a great habit to have. Anyway, we had a great day out at the Stonehenge, and my body was in perfect condition. Those guys really thought they had put one over on me. They apparently did not totally grasp the concept of dealing with a real American. Well, they did after that.

At this point, I was still trying to finalize plans for the purchase of that Volvo from Gothenburg. Peter was getting closer and closer to having enough money with which to travel, and the excitement was building. I was becoming more anxious each day to get going. Finally, a letter from my credit union came in, and, of course, I was thinking it was the final approval for the loan. That was not exactly what I found. The credit union considered me unemployed, even though I was just on a leave of absence, and Esther had changed jobs and locations, which should have had nothing to do with my loan application, as she was neither part of the loan application nor a part of my life anymore. The bottom line was the credit union had turned down the loan application, and it would take at least a month to process another one. All right, that idea was dead. My next chore was to cancel the flight to Gothenburg. Peter had intended to go with me; so, that meant we had to cancel both reservations and then wait for them to process the refund. We were on hold a bit longer, and now we were to be travelling a little differently than we had planned. It was all part of the continuing adventure.

When the travel service reimbursed us, and Peter was ready to go, we booked a coach (bus) from London to Cologne (Köln), Germany. We actually wanted to go directly to Munich, but could not get a direct connection. That was fine, however. I still had all that I was travelling with, which was quite a load, and Peter traveled a bit lighter. As I have indicated, I had not planned to travel all over Europe by bus or on foot. I had the old "wanderlust" in my heart and I did not really care how I moved about, just as long as I could see it all.

A little sacrifice can go a long way. I had already seen some wonderful things by this time; things most people never see in a lifetime. It was a long trip to Cologne, but very enjoyable nevertheless. We had plenty to eat and drink during the trip, and enjoyed just seeing everything along the way. We arrived in Cologne, got off the bus and headed for the local youth hostel, as we had joined the YHA (Youth Hostel Association) before leaving England. It was much less expensive to stay at the youth hostels than hotels. There was no comparison. When you travel on a budget that is the only way to go.

There are youth hostels all over Europe, not just for young people, but also for just about anyone who wishes to use them. I don't recall seeing extremely old people using them, but I was in my mid-thirties when I travelled, and no one questioned me. Most of the hostels were quite clean, considering how messy and sometimes dirty young people travelling can get. Hostels are accommodations for people on tight budgets to crash for the night and get a little something to eat as cheaply as possible. For those who do not mind having little to no luxuries or amenities, they are just fine. There are generally large rooms with bunk beds to sleep in, a dining room for breakfast (usually a continental breakfast) and dinners, if you care to eat there. The meals are not great (little more than bread, cold cuts, coffee and tea), but, when your resources are limited, then just about anything will do.

We had some friends in Limburg, as well as a couple of female companions we met on the bus from London, and we all got together for dinner at our friends' home. It was a very nice meal, and we brought wine to accompany the meal. They were both very nice people, and after speaking in German quite a while, I discovered the wife spoke beautiful English, and I commented on how well she spoke the language. She informed me there was good reason for that: she was English. Wow, I did feel silly, but she was speaking English with a German accent! She had been married to her German husband for about seven years, living in the small town of Limburg all that time, and she very seldom spoke English. That's why she was now enjoying speaking in her own native language. I needed the German practice and she needed the English practice. We all had a great evening together.

The year I was travelling, Europe experienced the coldest and snowiest winter it had had in the last sixteen years. The good news was there were not thousands of tourists everywhere we went, and that made it much nicer than a normal, summer tourist season would be. The other benefit was I was able to meet people from the southern hemisphere who were travelling, because it was their summer and their vacation season. I met many from Australia, South Africa and some from South America. I also noticed the Japanese like to travel in the winter. There were huge groups of Japanese in Germany all the time I was there. If you saw thirty Japanese in a group, you saw fifty cameras. Is that stereotyping? Yes, it probably is, but it is quite true at the same time.

The mode in which I travelled (alone) was also very interesting. Travelling with a group might be best for some, in that they have people they know with whom to do things and with whom to have a conversation. On the other hand, they might have a tendency to remain with the group and avoid expanding their horizons by meeting new people from different countries and cultures. That is the beauty of travelling alone. It might become a little lonely being alone all the time; so, that in itself is a natural motivation for meeting new people, and I can personally guarantee it works very well. I loved being by myself frequently, because I could do whatever I pleased, whenever I pleased without worrying about what someone else wanted to do and my infringing upon their ability to do the same.

Had I not been travelling alone, I would not have met Peter from England, Chris from Australia, and another Peter from the same city as Chris, Perth, and two other friends from South Africa, all with whom I did part of my travels. It was enlightening to meet people of other lifestyles and different parts of the world. That alone is an education. I suppose that is another reason I enjoyed military life so much. There were always opportunities for experiencing different cultures, and that is another form of growth and development as an individual, which gives a much broader spectrum of life in general.

Leaving Limburg, we bussed to Frankfurt, about an hour trip, where we were to board another bus for Athens, which was about a forty-hour trip. Peter and I gathered our food and drinks for the road trip (mostly bread, wine and cheese), and we were off to our next adventure. On our way south through Germany, we stopped at Munich and picked up another friend, Peter from Perth, and a little later, we found Chris from Perth.

We were then a group of four on our way to Greece. As good a group as we were, the more people there are in a group, the bigger the variety of opinions there is as to the most interesting things to see. The trip to Greece

Photo 18 - Athens, the Acropolis.

was not even my idea. Peter (my English buddy) came up with that idea. I had no intention at all of ever going to Greece. On the other hand, what other important things did I have to do? I was flexible, and it sounded like a bloody good idea. Why should I not see as much as possible while I had the opportunity?

The trip to Athens was for the most part uneventful. Most of the nicest areas to see we passed through during the night and didn't actually see much of it. Going into Yugoslavia, the customs officials detained us for a while. Had it not been for me, it might have been a very quick stop. I happened to be the only American on the bus. The customs people singled me out and took me into their back office for a little personal interrogation. The non-Americans all seemed to be very acceptable to them, but this American was of questionable character. Granted, I had grown a full beard at the time, as it was easier than shaving every day, and my passport showed a very "clean-cut American boy" appearance. I probably did not have the best of attitudes either, being the only

Photo 19 - Parthenon, Acropolis.

person on the bus whom they found necessary to hassle. I must have been the proverbial "ugly American." I personally thought I was the best looking of the group, however. I guess they didn't agree.

We finally made it to Athens, and then disembarked on foot to find some accommodations. While wandering aimlessly, we found an American Express travel office, and they directed us to a "cheap" hotel, which is what we were seeking. What we found was without a doubt a cheap hotel. It was the worst looking relic in town. This was Athens, and it really was full of ruins, and I am not entirely sure the hotel was not actually a part of ancient Greece. It was not all that far from the Acropolis and was in a similar condition. We did get what we were looking for, and that, too, proved to be something of an adventure. Besides that hotel, we actually did see some fantastic Greek ruins, including the Parthenon at the top of the Acropolis, overlooking all of Athens. I loved that part.

Photo 20 - Ruins at base of Acropolis.

As impressed as we all were with the ancient ruins, we were not overly impressed with the rest of Athens. We were not part of the jet set; so, we probably were not seeing what you would see in most of the Hollywood movies. We were definitely experiencing the real Athens, and that was not an entirely pretty picture. We decided to take a little trip across the water (Aegean Sea) to the island of Crete. We also heard we would probably not have to spend a great deal of money down there, and that had its appeal. We booked passage on a ferry, which was about a twelve-hour trip.

We all enjoyed the trip with the exception of my English friend, Peter, and he did not fare well with the water and the motion of the boat. He was sick from the start. He could not go below to sleep in a bunk, and I did not wish to do that anyway. I stayed out on deck

Photo 21 - Searching for sandy beaches on the south side of Crete.

with him. I love sleeping out under the stars anyway, and adding that to being on a boat was the best I could ask for. I did feel for Peter, but it did not spoil my trip.

We arrived at Khania on the north shore of Crete about 5:00 A.M., and just killed time for a couple of hours and had some breakfast. We discovered that, if we wanted to find any decent sandy beaches, we needed to go to the south side of the island. That appealed to us for two reasons. First, we loved the idea of taking advantage of the beach and swimming, weather and water temperature permitting. Secondly, we were thinking in terms of sleeping on the beach, as opposed to paying for a hotel.

Leave of Absence and Travel | 169

As I indicated, with four people, there was a variety of ideas floating about. Two of us thought it best to wait for a bus to take us to the south side, and the other two wished to hitchhike across the island. Peter and I preferred bussing. The two Aussies went off on their

Photo 22 - The gorgeous Mediterranean from our "sandy" beach on the south side.

own little adventure. We told them we would try to run into them later. We waited for another hour or a little more, and boarded a bus bound for a very small town called Chora Sfakion on the south side. After only ten or fifteen minutes, we were looking ahead through the front window of the bus, and we spotted Chris standing by himself on the road. I told the bus driver to stop for him, and Chris got on the bus. Somehow, he had lost the other Peter. They never caught a ride, and Pete ventured off somewhere. Chris then decided to stay with us.

We arrived on the south side in another hour or so, and we began to walk to find one of those elusive sandy beaches. We walked probably three miles east of Chora Sfakion, then back to the town and again another three or so miles west of the town. We finally found the closest thing we could find to a sandy beach and we

Photo 23 - Chris and Peter returning from another search for sandy beach.

settled in. We had to walk down some very steep, cliff-like inclines just to get down to the beach. We were carrying all of our belongings and had to use extreme caution. We were also very tired from all that walking with bags and full backpacks. The water was absolutely beautiful with its bright blue and green colors, contrasted with the snowy white foam of the breaking waves. Looking from the edge of the water back toward shore, we could see the caves cut in the cliffs by the ocean. We also had to explore them and we found them to be quite shallow, but they could offer cover in case of an unexpected storm. We were not exactly tuned into the Weather Channel.

The main problem with this beach was it was not sandy. The smallest grain of sand I could find was about a three-pound rock. That would not be conducive to a very comfortable sleep. While I began organizing our

Photo 24 - Chora Sfakion on south side of Crete.

campsite, Peter and Chris continued to search further up the beach for a better place. There was one spot I had seen earlier, which was a nice little cove, but it was a long and treacherous way down to the water, and there did not appear to be any caves or even a way to exit easily in case the tide came in. At least where we were it had both. We gave up on finding a better place and decided to sleep the night in our original location.

We had food and drinks for the evening and it seemed we were fairly well prepared for spending a quiet, comfortable (yes, rocky) night on the "beach." I love the relaxing, soothing sound of breaking waves on the beach. That alone can mesmerize me to sleep under normal circumstances. Our circumstances were probably not entirely normal, however. We really did try to sleep on those rocks, trying every possible way we could think of to get comfortable. It definitely was not working for me.

I finally gave up and decided to walk up the beach (over the rocks) for a while and to look up at the beautiful night sky over the Mediterranean Sea. It was a crystal-clear night and the stars were gorgeous. Very low on the horizon, across the sea, I could even see the Southern Cross. I was so fascinated with what I was observing I did not notice the tide coming in rapidly until a wave nearly broke over my legs. It occurred to me I had better head back to where the other guys were sleeping. We had already decided the safest place to be was in one of the caves up from the water line. We chose one that was a good distance from the water, just in case the tide did come in.

I arrived back to where I could see the cave just in time to watch a huge wave come up and wash right into that cave, submerging my two friends. The tide had come in just a tad bit faster and certainly in more volume than we had calculated. My friends survived it, but not without being totally soaked, as well as all of the sleeping bags, our backpacks and everything else we owned. Somehow, my camera equipment managed to avoid being submerged. I had put my camera bag up on a higher rock ledge.

When the others found I had been just a short distance from the cave when that wave came in, they were not at all happy with me. I was not on the top of their best friends list. I had tried to get to them, but didn't quite make it. I eventually convinced them I had not just stood by and watched them wash away with the tide. It had caught me as much off guard as it did them. I just happened to be in a better place at the time.

It took all the next day to dry things out on the beach. I stayed with all of our gear while Peter and Chris searched for a better beach once again. They were not successful and the next night we spent in a hotel in Chora Sfakion. We slept much more comfortably there and really did appreciate a nice reasonably soft and comfortable bed. We had to acknowledge also, how soft we really were. So much for the tough outdoorsy guys. We proved ourselves quite wimpy actually.

We bussed back to the north side of the island, met several other English speaking travelers, including our friend, Pete from Perth, whom we had lost the day before, and spent the day with them. We then stayed that night at the youth hostel in Khania and boarded the ferry back to Athens in the morning. Nothing had changed, and there was not much more we wanted to see in Athens, and in a couple of days, Peter and I headed back to Germany, while Chris was bound for Italy. He had purchased what was called a Euro-pass, which enabled him to travel anywhere in Europe with no further charges. He could go anywhere he wanted to for, I believe, ninety days without having to pay the fare. That was a great way to travel to see all of Europe, and I would love to have done the same, if that had been my focus. He planned to link up with me later in Germany.

Our route back to Germany was a bit different from the one going down to Greece, in that we came back through France. We even went through Paris, although we never made any significant stops. I never saw the Eifel Tower, not that it would have been any big deal for me. We went directly from there up to Antwerp, Belgium where we had to transfer to a train, which would take us back to Cologne. We could not get a train back to Limburg right away, and had to wait until the next morning when there was a train leaving at 6:30 A.M. We had to return to Limburg, as that is where we left a good deal of our extra baggage. We spent the whole day with our friends, the Lays, who fixed us a wonderful lunch and dinner that evening. Chris joined up with us again for a brief stay and left again to go on another of his own little journeys. About that time, Peter had run out of money, and had to return home to England, work and family. He had tried to find some work in Germany, but, because he could not speak German, he was out of luck.

It was time to make my move to Munich, where I intended to stay for a while. Almost immediately upon my arrival, I checked into a hotel I had read about in one of the books I had on Germany. It was reasonable in price. After unloading all of my gear and taking a quick snooze, I started walking around the city and just happened to run into a real live MacDonald's restaurant. Well, it had been a while since my last Big Mac, and I had to take a shot at it. Was I ever sorry for that decision. It was a matter of minutes before I began feeling nauseous and later became very sick. I decided my hotel room would be the best place to hang out that evening. I was terribly sick all night long and into the morning.

Chris had decided he would use Munich as his center of travel throughout the remainder of his time in Europe. As I, he, too, was a high school teacher. He had taken time off from work, just as I had. Knowing I was going to be staying in Munich, he thought it would be a good rest stop between trips, and I told him I had no objections. Had the hotel managers detected him, however, it could have cost both of us. We took the risk and it worked out quite well.

As reasonably priced as the hotel was at which I was staying, I did manage to find one just about as nice, but much cheaper, in that they charged by the week, rather than only by the day. That was the good news. The bad news was its name was the Vietnam Hotel. Considering my past military experience, I was somewhat hesitant, to say the least. It worked out just fine for a long time, until the day my Nikon F camera disappeared from my hotel room. I was more than just a little upset by that. I let them clearly know I knew exactly what had happened. I had definitely not left my room unlocked (at least I don't think so). Someone who had access to the room had taken the camera body from my case and left my valuable 200 mm telephoto lens, as well as my 28mm wide-angle lens. They only took the camera, along with one very nice lens. That was a huge loss to me. I loved that camera and had taken some fantastic pictures with it. I did eventually buy a new Nikon, but not nearly as nice. I was on a budget for a good reason.

My time in Munich was unique to me, in that I have never been in a single city with so many cultural activities. There is no limit to the entertainment. There is something for everyone. I went to concerts, including Fats Domino, the Munich Philharmonic Orchestra, a Nutcracker ballet, and others. There was every conceivable type of museum available. There was the Tierpark (equivalent to a city zoo), and there were botanical gardens and historical sites, as there were all over the country. I used to call Munich a large city with a small-town atmosphere. I considered it my favorite European city.

While wandering about town one day, I spotted a Baskin Robbins ice cream store. American ice cream definitely sounded like a great idea to me, in that the only ice cream I had been able to find up to that point was Italian Eis (ice cream), which wasn't bad, but reminded me of the old ice milk in the States. I did not like Italian ice cream that much, but it was better than none at all. The manager of this store indicated to me he was looking for another employee and he was interested in an American, especially one who could speak German, to add to the American cuisine. I bought my ice cream and ate it as I continued down the street. A day or so later I found they were quite serious about hiring me. I had an interview and the owner hired me almost right away. That job not only gave me extra cash, but also gave me a great opportunity to practice my German, which was one of the primary reasons why I wanted to be there. Learning a language in a classroom is valuable, but learning it in the native country is invaluable. There is no greater way to learn a language than to live it in a total emersion environment, and that is exactly where I was. It was great, and that was another mission accomplished.

I ended up working at Baskin Robbins for about two and a half months. I enjoyed most of the work and, though not extremely lucrative, it kept me going financially for a much longer time than I would have had without it, and it allowed me to make some purchases while there I would not have been able to make otherwise. I also had a great deal of contact with people, again giving me maximum exposure to the language and culture.

All the time I remained working for Baskin Robbins it was under the stipulation I would be getting an official work permit from the German Arbeitsampt (employment agency). They had originally given me every indication there would be no problem whatsoever attaining that permit. However, the reality of the situation was they were either lying through their teeth or the original person I talked to had no idea what was going on. They delayed and procrastinated, and then delayed some more. I was going through some ridiculous bureaucracy, which was to lead nowhere.

After over two months of working the ice cream shop, I was told by a supervisor at the employment agency I had no chance at all of ever getting a work permit. I was an American, and no one outside the European Economic Community (EEC) was authorized a work permit. It was just not going to happen. I never told them, of course, that I had actually been working for some time and I knew by then my days at Baskin Robbins were numbered. It was not more than a few days after notification that I would not get my permit when I heard someone from the Arbeitsampt was looking for me. I had only told them I had a job offer, not that I had begun working. Someone, however, had apparently "spilled the beans," because they seemed to know I was now an employee. It was about time to hit the road again. I really did not feel the need to visit a German jail at that time or even to pay a heavy fine.

I had wanted to see much more of Germany than I had been able to up to that point, and it did seem like immediately was the best time to take advantage of the opportunity to purchase a seventeen-day rail pass. They (the Arbeitsampt) had almost literally "run me out of town on a rail." Actually, I was just about ready to give up the ice cream business anyway, even though the owner of Baskin Robbins had offered me a manager position. His other manager was not working out well at all. It does seem like he should have been aware of the legalities, but it did not seem he had a major concern about the matter.

My boss was apparently not aware the Arbeitsampt was not going to give me a work permit. In any case, I had to quit, and I purchased my rail pass and was off to my travels again. In seventeen days, I saw thirty-five cities. I wasted no time in that little adventure, but I had a wonderful time seeing the country of the language I had been teaching for four years. It was enlightening and educational.

Chapter 8 – Transition to Real Life

When my seventeen days of German travel were complete, it was time for me to arrange to fly home. I flew from Frankfurt to Washington, DC, and eventually back to San Diego. It was back to the real world and my past life. The redeeming part was it was still early summer and I did not have to go back to work until early September when the fall semester of school resumed and my job. I enjoyed the rest of my summer. I was in a very nice apartment with a great pool area, and I made friends with nearly all the reasonably young single people in the complex. We all frequently socialized and had great times together.

One day well after the end of summer, after I had already gone back to work, there was a knock at my door. When I opened the door, I was startled to see my good old friend, Chris from Perth. Before we parted company in Germany, he had told me he intended to go home by way of the US, and I in turn invited him to come out to the west coast to visit, and I would show him around. He was obviously taking me up on the offer.

When I made that offer to Chris, I was actually thinking in terms of a few days, maybe a week at most. It would be six months before he was to leave, and that would be at my request. I liked Chris. He was a very nice guy and a very welcomed guest. I had said I would show him around, and, although I was now working again, as opposed to him, I still wanted to live up to my commitments and show him as much as I had time for, which ended up being quite a bit. I took him to the San Diego Zoo, the Wild Animal Park, Sea World, and, of course, all of the local beach areas. The weather was still good enough to take advantage of the interesting sights and activities around the area. The fact that I had recently purchased a brand new Nissan 280ZX, made it even more fun showing my friend around.

Time passed quickly, and summer changed to fall, which is not terribly significant in California, and on to winter. I thought the Grand Canyon would be a great thing for Chris to see: so, we planned a trip to Arizona. It was well into the winter season, and I had not ever seen the Grand Canyon by winter. It was a new experience for me, as well as my friend. After we had seen everything there was to see there, and it was truly spectacular as usual, we decided to go up to the White Mountains and to Flagstaff. Not far from there was the Snow Bowl ski area. We both decided that was a great idea. We were both novice skiers, but loved downhill skiing nevertheless.

After a great day on the slopes, we went down the mountain to Flagstaff for a nice meal and an evening of rest in our hotel room. On the way into Flagstaff, however, we spotted a nice sports bar, and decided to stop to shoot a little pool and have a beer or two. We ended up having dinner there, shooting pool and knocking off a couple of beers, and I am being honest about just a couple of beers in that length of time. When we left, the weather was bad with snow coming down. Visibility was poor and we really did not know exactly where that hotel was. We were looking carefully for it when I spotted it, but we were already passing it up. I drove for another block or so and made a U-turn. Almost immediately, I saw the old blinking red light behind me. I naturally figured I had made an illegal U-turn.

After the officer had checked my driver's license and registration, he asked me if I knew how fast I was going. I said, "Yes, about 47 miles per hour." He responded, "Do you know what the speed limit is here?" I said, "Well, the last one I saw posted was 45 miles per hour." "Well, you must have missed one of them, because it is 35." He had his head pretty close to the window, and he apparently detected the smell of alcohol. He asked me to get out of my vehicle and he was going to put me through a couple of roadside sobriety tests. I had no problem with that, having only had two beers with a meal in the last four hours. I was not even close to being drunk.

I already mentioned the weather, but I was just a dumb, southern Californian who never really thought about the outside weather elements. It was very cold, and I did not bother putting on a jacket. I just got out of my car and was ready to do whatever he directed. He first asked me to take the old "touch the nose with your index finger" trick. I had the shakes from the cold so badly I did not do well on that test. The next request was for me to walk a straight line. The cold got to me again. I actually did a nice little stagger in something less than a straight line. That did not quite do it for the Flagstaff officer. He put me into the back of his cruiser, which was the "cage."

No one can understand how intimidating that is unless he or she has been there. I was guilty of nothing, but I was in the back of a police cruiser on my way to the police station. The thoughts going through my mind were that everyone looking my way was seeing a criminal in the back of a police car going off to jail. The officer was only taking me to the police station for a breath analyzer test, as he did not carry one in his police car. It turned out negative, of course, and the police were very nice and apologetic about having to take me downtown, and they gave me a ride back to my car. I chalk it up as another experience. That really is about the closest I have ever come to being arrested. That should be good news. I think so.

Chris was a good houseguest, as well as a good friend. However, even a good friend can get on your nerves after a certain length of time. Chris was always willing to help in any way he could, just to make things easier on his host. He not only took care of his own messes, his own dishes and his own laundry, but he even volunteered to do my laundry. He once picked up all my laundry from the hamper, dumped it all into the washer, and decided that his red sweatshirt also needed washing, and proceeded to throw that in. The color of my underwear from that point forward was pink. I'm sorry, but being an infantry, airborne, ranger, I, Captain Macho at the time, would not allow myself to wear pink underwear. I mean, I did have a certain amount of self-respect. I had something of an image to maintain, and pink underwear would not exactly enhance that aspect of my life. It was probably a false image anyway, but really, denial has always worked for me, and I was quite happy with it.

One day Chris asked to borrow my iron to iron his jeans. How many people iron jeans? Then again, who was I to question that? Why not? Of course, he could borrow my iron. That was an extremely expensive iron, which I had just recently purchased. Back then, I did use an iron a great deal. I always wanted to look my best, and I spared no expense at getting a nice one to do a nice job.

While Chris was ironing his jeans, he was not paying much attention to what he was doing, and proceeded to iron right over the zipper, as though his zipper were wrinkled. That did not do my new iron any good whatsoever. It put a huge, deep scratch right down the center of it, so deep it actually snagged on the clothing I attempted to iron. Need I say, I was not a happy camper over that one? He was very helpful, but to the point of distraction. I loved the guy, but what a pain in the "arse."

After a full six months had passed, and Chris was still hanging about, I became very direct with him. After many subtle hints it might be time for him to go home, that there may actually be people who miss him, I finally confronted him by saying, "Chris, go home!" I told him to try his best not to take it personally, although, yes, it was quite personal. We had reached a point where, although his stay had been very nice, it had also been a bit over-extended. Six months had been a very long visit. He did have to agree with that, and he soon departed and we were still on very good terms. Our friendship did last, although it was not terribly long before we lost contact. We both had renewed lives to live, and it was time for both of us to get on with those lives.

I continued to enjoy the fun times with all of the other people of the apartment complex. Most of us were single, and did a fair amount of socializing, especially on the weekends. It was just a short time before Chris left that the granddaughter of my apartment managers and their daughter showed up on a visit from Michigan. They actually arrived on New Year's Eve, and there was a party someone threw to which the whole apartment complex was invited. It was not unusual back then for me to have a bit too much to drink, particularly on New Year's Eve. After having consumed a good deal of heavy-duty punch that evening, I was looking across the room at an extremely attractive young lady. She seemed to be a little fuzzy, but there was little doubt in my mind I wanted to meet her and find out who she was. I had never seen her before and we had not yet been introduced.

The granddaughter's name was Debbie. Debbie was not terribly impressed with me that night. That insignificant fact did not discourage me, however. After all, I was not in my right mind. She was quite clear headed, having had nothing alcoholic to drink, and she had little tolerance for someone who was not clear headed. My speech may have been somewhat unclear at the time, and, of course, I merely thought there could have been some miscommunication between the two of us. The next day I had every intention of working on that minor problem.

It really did take a while to convince her I really was genuine in my feelings for her. I would never go so far as to say it was love at first sight, because that was by no means the case. I think I really was more lusting after her than anything, particularly that first night I saw her. It genuinely bothered me to see one other young man, who was actually a friend of mine, trying to take advantage of her. I knew what he was after, and he did not try to hide it. His name was Hank.

Hank was from the Netherlands. He was a very nice guy, but, when it came to the girls, he had little respect for them. He used to brag he had had intimate relations with every girl in the apartment complex, including many of those who were married. He really thought himself to be the proverbial stud. When he invited Debbie to get naked, and join him in the shower, that was pretty much it for me. Debbie even said to him, "Hank, I don't even know you." He came back with, "What better way can you think of to get to know me?" She declined. I told him to back off before I had to let him have it, and he was eight or ten inches taller than I was. That made no difference to me. I hardly knew Debbie, but I really thought she deserved better than that.

I think Debbie did appreciate that, but she was still not sure she trusted me entirely. I opened the car doors for her and was a gentleman all the way, and she did not know quite how to react to that. She was thinking there must be some ulterior motives for all those actions. Little did she know that was just my nature. It took a couple of weeks to convince her. Then, when she found out I was a Vietnam veteran, she backed off again. She really had some preconceived ideas about Vietnam vets. As far as she knew, all Vietnam veterans were potheads or had scrambled brains and were crazy. I may have been a bit crazy, but it was not a result of Vietnam.

Deb and I began doing more things together and we got to know one another very well in a short time. We began to grow on each other more and more each day. There was a span of nearly fifteen years between us, and many thought I was "robbing the cradle" and it would never last. Oddly enough, it never seemed to be a problem for us. Just about eight months later, we were married and have been now for thirty-four years. Something must have been right.

Deb and I began our family almost right away. Although she was only twenty-one, I was already thirty-six just before our wedding, and I did not really want to wait around forever to begin having children. As it is, I became a father at an older age than my mother was when she became a grandmother. She was a thirty-six-year-old grandmother, and I was thirty-seven when I first became a father. With regard to "robbing the cradle," I suppose the cradle did rock a few times early in our marriage, but it never fell. We made it through just fine. "Love conquers all."

About fourteen months after our wedding, our family began to grow, beginning with a boy, followed by another boy, followed by another boy. Oh boy, what a trip that was through the years, but a very enjoyable one. Deb and I like to think we were very good parents, although we sometimes have second thoughts about some of the things we did in their growing-up years. Probably all parents later in life have thoughts about how they could have been better about some of the decisions they made with regard to child raising. We are no exceptions. We were not staunch disciplinarians with our children, and yet we cut our boys very little slack when it came to their behavior outside the house. Some of the things we did to maintain order and control might have landed us in jail today, but it did seem to work very well at the time.

Whenever we travelled, which was quite frequently, we always carried a wooden spoon in the car. Now, we never intended that spoon to be an implement of physical abuse, nor did we ever use it as such. Most people understand it is a Biblical principle from the Old Testament not to "spare the rod" when it comes to disciplining children. Our church at the time believed in that principle, and so did we, as parents. I still do. Dr. Spock was never one of my favorite people. The wooden spoon was merely an implement of attention getting when required, and it was always just a quick, little snap, and never even close to a beating.

With Mom and Dad in the front seat and three young boys in the back, it would have been difficult, if not impossible, to get their attention when they were in the midst of battle in the rear by just saying, "Oh, my little cutie pies, I would like you to be much quieter, if you don't mind." That would have been much more polite, I'm sure, but perhaps not so practical. In other words, it would never have worked, contrary to some people's beliefs today. No, a quick, little sting on the leg from that spoon would get their attention right away, and indicate clearly to them this is not appropriate activity in the back seat while we are driving. They did not much like it, but then again we were not doing it to please them either.

Deb did not much like the wooden spoon for the boys, even when we felt the need to use it, and later thought it was perhaps a bit harsh. This is just one place where we have to agree to disagree. I still think it was an effective tool, and it does not seem to have affected the emotional stability of any of the boys. We talk about it at times today, and even laugh about it. Even though they did not like it, they see the value it had.

Some of my readers may well cringe at this one, but I really have to relate one incident in particular where we were trying to instill in Brent, our middle son, how inappropriate his attitude was at the time, and the consequences of behaving that way. Brent was just a little different from the other two boys, in that he had a little tougher time than the other two in getting through his "terrible twos." Most children go through that stage, but Brent made a transition from "terrible twos" to "terrifying threes" to quote Deb.

Brent was three years old, I believe, when he was having a particularly bad day, and it just so happened some of the family was visiting, and we decided we were going out to lunch. Deb and I always agreed on a very adamant policy with our children that they would, under no conditions, act up in a restaurant in such a way as to make it unpleasant for anyone in that restaurant. Rather than that happening, we would escort the young man out of the restaurant immediately and take care of business. We would also not allow them to ruin our meal or time together.

On this particular day, our little Brent was not being pleasant. We were thinking seriously about leaving him home with his Grandpa, who didn't feel like going anyway. However, everyone wanted Brent to go along, and we took him. We pulled up into the parking lot of the restaurant, and he was still displaying an attitude. We told him to straighten up or he was not going to have lunch with us, and we were not the kind of parents who tried to bluff their children. We meant what we said most of the time. Well, he immediately got the sympathy of Grandma and Aunt Vicky. Vicky automatically leaned into the back seat, being all wonderful and nice to Brent, and said, "Oh, Brent, come on, Sweetie, let's come out and have a nice lunch together." As she was encouraging him to get out of the car, he reared back and punched her in the stomach. She backed off and yelled, "Well, you rotten kid!" and pushed him back into his car seat. We did not take Brent into the restaurant that day.

I parked the car right in front of a big window of the restaurant where I had spotted an empty table. The car was also under a tree with the car windows partially rolled down. We left Brent in the car while we all went into the restaurant and sat down for lunch right by that big window. We kept a very close eye on him, and he had us well in view during our entire lunch. That was very difficult for us to do, but I can hardly express how effective that was. He watched us consume that entire meal from the car, and he did not eat lunch that day. He never again acted that way when going out for a meal. The bottom line is it worked, cruel as it may seem to some. We were serious about that policy, and that certainly proved it to Brent, as well as the other two. In today's world, I would not recommend that strategy, as parents would likely go to jail.

We had another incident that may raise many eyebrows. We were on another of our trips across country to Michigan when the boys were becoming unruly in the back seat. They were just restless and doing what boys do, primarily fighting, as well as having fun, but they were way out of control. After repeatedly telling them to settle down, nothing seemed to be working. We went off the main highway and found a very secluded road that had little or no traffic. We stopped the car, and told the boys, "Get out!" They, of course, just looked at us with faces of disbelief. Their eventual response was, "What do ya mean, get out?"

"What does it seem like I mean? Get out and start walking."

"Start walking? How far are we supposed to walk?"

"I don't know yet. How about until I get tired? How about until you walk out whatever is in you to make you continue to act this way? You guys have been sitting too long and need to work off some energy. This is a great way to do it; now start walking."

They began their little trek. At first, they saw humor in it, laughing and giggling. They played, almost making fun of what we were making them do. Then the humor began to fade a bit. They eventually were getting tired and bored with this activity. They wanted back in the car. That's not the way I saw it. I finally gave in, but only with their assurance things would be much better the rest of the way. They lived up to their agreement for the most part, and we enjoyed the rest of the trip. Our boys were wonderful kids, but they did have to know a few rules and be able to follow them.

To some degree, raising our three boys reminded me of my own life growing up and attempting to make it to manhood. They had their share of accidents and minor injuries, as I did, but many of their accidents, I have to admit, were my own fault, particularly when it came to Craig, my oldest. I am not entirely sure today how he has managed to make it as far as he has. As parents, we all know we try our very best to insure undesirable things do not happen to our children. We also know, as hard as we try, things do not always work out exactly as planned. Things just have a tendency to happen.

You can plainly see I am setting up justification for what I am about to relate. Denial really does go a long way. When Craig was still an infant, and at that time, an only child, I sometimes carried him in a way with which some family members disagreed. It was the "football carry," and the two of us seemed perfectly comfortable with it. I had at least as much emotional connection with my precious son as any quarterback has for his precious football, maybe more! Yes, it was more.

There was one time, when he was a little older, and I was not using the football carry, Craig and I had a little accident together. He was still an infant and I had him in a receiving blanket. Deb and I early in our marriage enjoyed "window shopping" for houses. We loved to just go out and dream a little, looking at homes we could not afford, but looking to the future. I had a new pair of shoes that had crepe soles, and I was coming down the carpeted stairway of one of the homes, carrying Craig on my right shoulder. My foot caught on the carpet and I lost my balance.

As my body fell forward, I was very much aware of my son and what was coming, as I held him in my arms. I knew I was going down hard, and I had to avoid injuring him at all cost. As I fell, I twisted my body so I would hit on my back, with him on my chest, and avoid crushing him. I hit hard, and, as I did, my poor little son shot out of the receiving blanket like a cannon ball. I thought I had him, but I was very wrong. He sailed down the remaining couple of steps to the floor below, well ahead of me. Thank the Lord he was not injured, and I was extremely relieved to find he had no bumps or bruises at all on him. I had a few of my own, of course, but that is always par for the course.

Now and then, especially when Mom was not around, we would tend to play a little too rough. Well, Deb, quite pregnant with Brent at the time, was away somewhere, and my son and I were alone. We were having great fun, and I began to run through the house, carrying him on my right shoulder. Just as we were about to run through the door into the kitchen, he decided to lean right. Wham! Craig's head collided with the wall next to the door. Wow, what a crack that was! I thought I had killed him for a moment. The volume of his crying dispelled that idea quickly. I felt horrible about having done that, but it really did not appear I had caused much damage.

While Craig was still a toddler, we went off to Michigan, and, while there, we went up to Mackinaw Island, right where the upper and lower peninsulas meet. It is a gorgeous little island with some great history, including an old Army fort, and fantastic shops, which include the famous Mackinaw Island fudge shops. The island has a beautiful road all the way around it, right along the shoreline, as well as roads through the center, the best part being no motorized traffic allowed anywhere. All vehicles are horse-drawn or peddled.

It was a great trip, and, while we were there, we decided to rent bicycles to ride around the island. I had been carrying Craig everywhere in a backpack, and bicycling would be no different. It was just before this trip that I had carried him all through Washington, DC, in the same backpack. Anyway, off we went on our bikes, and we really were having a great time, enjoying every moment of it, admiring the Mackinaw Bridge and the other islands off in the distance. The warm sun and cool breeze of the lake made it even better.

As we rode, Craig was thrilled with the outdoors and all that went with it, just as we were. He was so excited he could hardly sit still, and, in fact, took a giant leap straight up and so hard that he left the backpack. Fortunately, with Deb in back of me, and Craig on my back, the three of us riding a tandem bike, she was able to snatch him by the leg as he went up, bringing him back down into the "saddle." Had it not been for Deb's quick snag, Craig would have been in the street, and who knows what the result of that would have been? Craig had his own guardian angel on that trip. His parents were obviously not in complete control. However, Deb did spend the rest of that bike trip prepared to grab Craig's legs, rather than just clinging to the handlebars of the bike.

While living in southern California, Deb and I became very involved in our church. We eventually became part of the leadership. When our wonderful pastor died of a heart attack, the much younger youth pastor became the senior pastor. He was a true and faithful man of God, and at the same time, he always had a great sense of humor and was frequently quite mischievous. He had been a notorious prankster before his taking over as senior pastor, and still had a hard time getting past that tendency. He was a kid at heart.

One evening we received a phone call from someone who identified himself as Sergeant Smith from the San Diego Police Department. He said he was investigating the disappearance of one of my students at Torrey Pines

High School and wanted to know if I had any information as to her whereabouts. There was no doubt in my mind it was Pastor Doug, particularly choosing a name like Smith. I decided to play along with his game for a while.

I said, "Yes, officer, you have nothing to worry about. I did snag her, and she is safely locked in the trunk of my car. I'll be sure to return her when I think the time is right." The person on the other end of the line just paused for a few moments and repeated the first part of his message. "Sir, this is Sergeant Smith from the San Diego Police Department, and I certainly hope that you are taking this seriously, because your comment is certainly being taken seriously. I am looking for...(stating the name of the student) who has been missing since yesterday." There is no way Pastor Doug could have known the student's name, and that was not good for me. I was feeling just a little uncomfortable at that moment. As a last attempt to hear what I needed to hear, I said, "Come on, Doug; please tell me that this is you." The officer once again, and for the last time, identified himself.

My next comment was, "Oh, crap! This must mean that I am in a heap of trouble, right, officer?"

"Yes, sir, it would certainly mean that you have some explaining to do." I was in a bit of shock as I realized this was actually for real.

I then confirmed I knew the student, and offered as much information as I could. I remained a suspect, however, until she was finally located. I guess I was lucky I didn't end up in jail for that little episode. It was funny later on when that young lady was discovered to have just run off somewhere without telling her parents. I did make a very big deal of it to my wonderful Pastor Doug. I never let him forget that one. I blamed him for the whole thing, of course. He was much better about refraining from pranks after that. It was probably a good lesson for both of us.

Although I do wish part of my focus to remain on challenging risks, perhaps followed by failures, which lead to successes, I cannot overlook opportunities to share some very humorous situations with you. There was a situation that took place in a home in Encinitas, California, the home of one of the members of our church, during a Wednesday night Bible study. My good friend, Peter, was leading the study that night. We were all sitting in a large room, and there were probably twenty of us in attendance.

The subject for the study was very serious and important. It was from the Book of Revelation, and had to do with the end times. We were captivated by the dynamics of Peter's presentation, as he was doing an excellent job of it. At one point in the middle of his study, a huge fly buzzed in and was pestering all of us. Without warning, the fly made a dive at my face and flew right up my nose. Terribly startled, my head flew back and I gave a hard blow out of my right nostril, holding the left side shut, and the fly came out as though blown from a pellet gun. It continued its flight across the room where it flew directly into Peter's mouth as he was speaking! Hardly flinching, Peter spit the fly out of his mouth and continued speaking as though nothing unusual had ever happened.

During that horrible, yet hilarious, time Debbie and Peter's wife, Bee, were sitting together on a couch just across from where I was. They had witnessed that whole sequence of events, and finally could not contain themselves, and burst out laughing. Peter was terribly serious, explaining the end times and the whole impact of that, while Debbie and Bee were laughing so hard they had tears in their eyes. They were totally out of control and had to leave the room. It was a memory that will never lapse. That was a very serious moment, which turned into a hilarious outcome. It was beautiful, and did prove in my mind that God does indeed have a great sense of humor. Peter never even knew what happened until the end of the evening when we all had to explain the whole thing. Only then did he understand what the commotion was all about.

During my tenure as a high school teacher, I did extend my duties a bit beyond the classroom. I was never terribly fond of the whole idea behind unions, yet at the same time, I saw the necessity for one in the teaching profession. The school board I worked with was never in favor of improving the status of its teachers. We had to fight long and hard battles for every benefit we ever received, not terribly different from most school systems. We were a school district in a very wealthy area, but the money, just like most other districts, was extremely tight. There were few alternatives other than relying on the union for help.

Shortly after I became a part of the union, which at the time was a very liberal organization that believed in most of what I did not support, that I felt forced to look at the big picture and what the union could do for my chosen profession. After several years, I became the district grievance chairperson. There were a number of significant and valid grievances in our district, and I was then the man who had to support those needy teachers who were fighting for their professional lives. In the process, of course, I did not win new friends among school administrators. They were trying to find ways of getting rid of the teachers they no longer had a need for, and I was trying to save those teachers from unfair practices. It did not help my quest for furthering my own career, but I was able to help others. That made me feel much better about what I was doing.

As the years passed, I lost more ground, as my new principal felt my teaching techniques were not according to what he believed were best. I had less structure than what he wanted to see. He claimed I did not exercise enough classroom management. He even forced me to take special courses in classroom management. I could have argued forever, but it would have been in vain.

There was very little those classes presented I did not know, but had chosen not to use.

Just as any other profession, the teaching profession had its wonderful aspects, as well as those that were considerably less than wonderful. I had fun with my students, and most of them made my job rewarding and meaningful. I sometimes claim I never really grew up, as it took me twenty-four years to get out of high school, including my own four. Honestly, my students kept me thinking, and probably even looking younger. When youth surrounds you, it tends to permeate your whole being. I think I became something of a product of my environment.

Most teachers will attest to the fact that it is a profession that, if you do a very bad job of it, you will undoubtedly hear about it. On the other hand, if you do an outstanding job at something, you may never hear you have been successful. Very seldom will students or parents come back to you to tell you how well you have done. That is not a complaint, but rather an observation. There are exceptions, however. Having been an English teacher, I was always putting comments on student papers, mostly having to do with writing mechanics, but often the students had things to express in their papers I felt needed my personal input. I have to admit my comments were not always without a personal opinion.

I was out at a Billy Graham revival at the San Diego Chargers stadium one night, and suddenly a young man came running up to me and gave me an unbelievably warm greeting. I recognized him as one of my old students from several years back. He related to me a comment I had put on one of his papers that had turned his whole life around. I had no idea at the time it would have any impact whatsoever on him. I learned that night I had affected a student's life in a very positive way, and that made everything that might have ever seemed negative about that profession disappear. Things like that can make everything worthwhile and truly meaningful. I can hardly express the wonderful feeling of accomplishment I had after that meeting. It was far greater than the revival itself.

Now and then, there were things that happened in my school, and even in my own classroom, that were less than pleasant. That school was built in 1974, the same year I began my teaching career and tenure at that school. It was designed with the 70s idea of an open classroom environment. That is, none of the classrooms in the main building had any doors. They all had three walls, and, where the fourth wall would have been was open to the hallway. I think the idea was for students never to have a closed in, claustrophobic feeling of the normal classroom. It also meant any activity in the hallway was an automatic distraction for the students, and any noise at all from other classrooms would be distracting. All classes are, of course, not noiseless. That would usually include my own classes.

The open classroom environment also left the classrooms vulnerable to just about anything, including theft, vandalism and students wandering the halls without permission and just wanting to visit. I walked into my classroom early one morning and detected a very strong odor hanging in the air. Upon further inspection, I discovered a very large deposit of human feces in my trashcan. Ugh! I discovered a completely new definition of being "shit-canned." As bad as that sounds, it was not the only time it happened. We had a viewing room right off the auditorium, which was just large enough for a single class to watch a movie. One of the times I took my class into that room, I discovered the same thing had happened there. We had a student who had a psychological disorder, and we never found him (presumably male). On both occasions, I felt terrible about notifying the custodians about their next obligation. They took it very well, however.

Then there was the time one of my little gems (students) decided to kick a hole in the wall of my portable classroom. I did not actually see him do it, but several of my students did. I cornered the kid and told him he would have to take the consequences of that action. He just looked me in the eye and said, "Hey, prove that I did it." I responded with, "You know you did it, the class knows you did it and I know you did it. What more do we need?" I told him that, if he wanted to take it higher, we could go there, and I would just turn it over to the principal. He told me to go ahead and do that, but I wouldn't get far. That was a challenge to me, of course, so, that's what I did.

When the principal of the school found out who it was who did the dirty deed, his response to me was, "John, forget it. Just drop it; let it go." I couldn't believe he was really saying that. I told him I really needed his support, and I could not believe he was not giving it to me. When I questioned him about that, he informed me the kid's father was a "big-time" corporate lawyer in California, and he was not going there with this little situation. I told him, if nothing were done about it, then I would be perceived as the incompetent teacher with no classroom discipline, lacking in classroom management skills. I would end up being the bad teacher, and the kid would get away with proverbial murder. My wonderful principal just shrugged and dismissed the whole thing.

I was more than a little angry. I immediately went to the district superintendent and requested a transfer to the other high school in the district for the coming semester. There was not another English teaching position available at the other high school, but there was one coming up at one of the junior high schools. Although I reluctantly took the position, it did not work out well for me. I hated teaching at that level, and it was not long afterward I submitted my resignation from the district, and that was pretty much the end of my full-time teaching career. That was definitely a huge risk to take, in that I did not have another job on which to fall back. I presumed something else would magically present itself to me. I mean, I was such an outstanding teacher there would have to be a huge demand for me, right? Well, of course, right.

I worked long and hard at that profession, and loved what I was doing. My work hours, as many teachers will attest to, ran much longer than the six and a half or seven hours each day on campus. I spent many long hours correcting papers and evaluating student work, lesson plan preparation, union work and classroom management work, as well as Army Reserve or California National Guard responsibilities, and, of course, my early morning runs at least three or four days each week, and all of that was probably a very good reason for never getting enough sleep.

With no more than three and a half or four hours of sleep each night, I was dragging most of the time. Even when I took my family out for entertainment, I would always have a folder full of school-related work to do, which had to be very irritating to them at times. I even took my family to a professional hockey game in San Diego one night and was correcting papers during the game. My boys were not overly pleased with that one. I heard one of them say, "Mom, is Dad really correcting papers now?" I really was watching the game at the same time.

One day, while driving home from work at about 3:30 in the afternoon, my normal time for going home, I fell asleep at the wheel of my little Hyundai. I remember opening my eyes just before impact with the telephone pole. It was too late to react in any way. I slammed into the pole at full force, which broke in half. I blacked out for just a moment before looking down at the floor and seeing my right leg at a very unusual angle. My foot was at a right angle to the rest of my leg. It did not look good.

I had never had a broken leg before, but I was quite certain that this time was an exception. It was indeed a very significant fib-tib break. The impact was such that my seat belt had broken and my upper body had slammed very hard into the steering column, just bruising me, with no serious injuries, but alarming the paramedics when they looked at it. I had extracted myself from the car by lifting my right leg up and out of the door on the driver side and standing on my left leg. I was not sure my car would not catch on fire, and I did not want to be in it if it did. I was not in much pain, and I acted as though I were not hurt very badly. I found out later I had about 70,000 volts of electricity over my head all that time, and it could well have fried me. I guess I was fortunate in many ways.

There were a few minor repercussions from that incident. The first little problem that arose was a misunderstanding of who the injured person really was. Shortly after my arrival at the hospital, one of the hospital personnel called my wife and scared the daylights out of her by describing my injuries in medical terms about which most normal, non-medical people would have no clue. My leg was not just broken, but rather "deformed." I did not just have scratches and bruises, but rather "contusions and abrasions." My chest was not just bruised, but there was "a contusion of the chest with possible heart damage."

After that brief conversation with the hospital, she thought I was probably right on the edge of death. She was thinking maybe she'd like to see me once again before I "checked out." She also had to make a phone call to her friend, the pastor's wife, Sandy, to take her daycare kids for her so she could go to the hospital to say her good-byes.

A good friend, and the father of one of the day care kids, just happened to share my first name, John. John's wife, Denise, Deb's good friend, passed away a few weeks before my accident, and Deb began watching their little deaf son right after the death of his mother. While talking to Sandy, whom she called, Deb told her John had been in an accident and she wanted to go there to be with him. Sandy thought she meant John, the father of the day care boy. She told Deb that was very thoughtful, but she would be happy to go down to check on John. Deb then told her it might even be a nicer gesture if she could go down to be with her own husband in his time of need. Only then did it occur to Sandy that I was the injured John. Later on it was funny, but not to Deb at the time.

The doctors did some significant surgery on my leg, putting in some screws and brackets that remain today. It has been a little difficult to get through security people at the airports since that operation, but other than that, I have never had much trouble with the leg. The doctor told me at the time, if I ever had problems with the hardware in my leg, he would be happy to go back in and remove it. I never saw the necessity for that. One operation was quite sufficient for me.

That accident seemed important at the time, in that I was on crutches for two or three months and in a cast for six months, which did slow my pace for a while. That little incident could have ended my life, but, once again, worked out extremely well. Another thing that was interesting was the telephone pole I broke in two, simply separated, and the upper section came straight down vertically, so it was just parallel with the lower section, like two poles standing side by side. It was quite remarkable actually. It must have been those angels still at work. In any case, what could have been my last big checking out moment of life turned out very much the opposite.

I mentioned earlier I used to get up bright and early in the morning, long before getting ready for work. It was my time for my daily run. I would be up no later than 3:30 A.M. and run for five miles. My course was on level ground for a while, then downhill, level for a couple of miles, then back up the hill for a mile or so, followed by the end being level again. It was a great run during which I got super cardiovascular exercise, I was able to think clearly without interruption, and I just thoroughly enjoyed it. It even felt good physically. One morning during the early part of my run, I encountered the biggest coyote I had ever seen before. He really was the size of a normal wolf. I was running on the sidewalk at the time, when I looked up and I was not more than ten yards in front of that brute.

I stopped dead in my tracks and we just glared into each other's eyes. Neither of us was ready to give way to the other. All right, enough of the drama. I'm lying. I was not at all reluctant to give way. I very slowly backed off, not to startle him. I made a very wide path around where he was standing. I use the masculine here just for simplicity, and the fact that I cannot imagine a female being that large. Neither did I get close enough to check it out.

The old reference to being a "live coward" as opposed to a "dead hero" really applies well here. It was, however, a great experience and a wonderful encounter with nature in the raw. It was one to remember, and right in the city no less. We could also apply the old quotation, "Discretion is the better part of valor" here, as it helped me once again to be successful in my pursuit of life. I avoided a potentially very hazardous confrontation with nature. I think we were both pleased to walk away from one another. It's tough to speak for the coyote, but I can, without hesitation, speak for myself.

It was also during this time in the life of my family that we underwent some serious changes in our lifestyle. When Deb and I were first married in 1980, I had been teaching for six years, and we were in a good financial situation. There were just the two of us with very few responsibilities. We lived in a very nice apartment above the horseracing track in Del Mar, California, and there was very little we could not afford to do. I had that nice little sport car, which, as soon as Deb became pregnant, we traded in for a more reasonable piece of transportation, but, before that, we took some very nice trips in that car.

One of those trips was when we decided to go white water rafting down the Colorado River. We drove to Las Vegas, and after a one-night stay and some actual winnings in a casino, which nearly paid for our trip, we headed out to the airport where we flew in a small airplane out to the Grand Canyon. From that very small desert airport, we flew by helicopter down into the canyon. From that departure point, we traveled three days on an eighteen-man raft down river. What a trip! It was fantastic by any standards.

Looking up from the river to the top of the Grand Canyon gives a far different perspective than one can ever get from looking down into it from the rim. There is no question about how majestic it is, looking down from the rim of the canyon to the Colorado River thousands of feet below. Looking up from the river, however, can also take your breath away. It is one of the most awesome sights imaginable.

On our journey, we went through a variety of transitions of the river. It would be very calm, smooth water for a long time, which was very relaxing, peaceful and beautiful. Then the water would begin to churn and become rougher and rougher until the raft would literally shoot skyward and crash back into the white water. On one of those awesome and exciting occasions, we actually lost one of the rafters off the end of the boat, an old man in his eighties. He was sitting on one of the footlockers filled with our supplies, mostly food.

The locker was secured, but the strap broke loose and both the locker and the man went off the back. It was icy cold water, and the poor man looked like he would either drown or freeze to death. The crew reacted very quickly and pulled the man out of the water. He came through it quite well, considering his age. We lost a few supplies and food, but it could have been much worse. That trip was better than the wildest of roller coaster rides. No amusement park I have ever experienced can challenge that kind of exhilaration. After the wild rapids, we would be back into calm, quiet tranquility, just as quickly as we left it.

As the first day neared its end, we had to look for a good place to stop and camp for the night. Our selection was an island in the middle of the river. It may have connected to one side of the river and might have been a peninsula, but it looked like an island. Anyway, we had visitors that night. Along with the humans who were with us, we also found we had uninvited reptiles who wanted a nice warm spot to sleep for the night.

One of our visitors was a rattlesnake, which did not create the most comfortable environment for us. One of the crewmembers of the expedition was able to grab the snake and escort him far away from our camp. Our next visitor was a big fat Gila monster that wandered into our campsite. He was huge, with those beady eyes and about a four-inch forked tongue waving around in our direction. He had our attention with little effort on his part. We encouraged him away from us, but sleeping well that night was not consistent with the situation, at least not for Deb. I actually thought he was kind of cool. Then again, I'm not always the brightest star in that beautiful, desert night sky.

Deb was really funny that night. I can't help but think of the movie title "Night of the Iguana," except we had a Gila monster instead, which could be worse than an iguana. That beast did make her more than a little uneasy, but the thought of a rattlesnake curling up inside her sleeping bag was nearly too much for her. The raft crew had given us Army issued ammunition cans in which to carry our personal items. Deb made me place those cans, along with a barricade of large rocks all around where our heads would be while we slept.

We must understand this was Deb's first encounter with rattlesnakes, having come out of Michigan where there are a few, but not nearly like the southwest. Her logic told her the snake was so far away, after the crew member had taken it far from the campsite, that it would be too tired upon its return to climb over the rocks. Therefore, he would go around her rock-surrounded sleeping bag and go into mine instead. Later on, she learned the snake would probably have been looking for the warmth of the rocks, but that was later. The result of all this was she did feel more secure, and that was what was most important. We woke up the next morning with no snakes in our bags. Obviously, Deb was absolutely right. Those ammo cans did stop the snakes in their tracks. (That's no cliché. Snakes do make tracks.) It is the only logical conclusion, right?

Chapter 9 – Family Trips, an Extended Adventure

Debbie and I remained in California for another fifteen years after we were married. As we raised our boys, we placed visits to Michigan very high on our priority list in order for them to get to know Deb's side of the family. We were able to drive across country four or five times during that period. We also made it a point to drive a different route on each trip. In that way, we were all able to see the vast majority of our country.

The boys had more experience in travelling as children than most adults ever have. They were able to see most of the remarkable natural phenomena throughout the country, as well as most of the common tourist attractions. We very seldom set a specific route and stuck to it. We would gather as much information as possible about each state, so we would not leave important things behind and maybe never have a chance to see them again. We frequently went far out of our way to see things that might be of interest to all of us.

The shortest route possible to northern Michigan was about 2700 miles, which would include five of us travelling. That was a trip we took at least twice with our very small Hyundai, and we very seldom stayed in hotels for the night. We would generally sleep on the road and just keep rolling until we reached our destination. There were, of course, some exceptions to that routine. The real exception was there was seldom a routine. We were always spontaneous. We enjoyed that very much, and the trip was often much longer than that 2700 miles. We also enjoyed experiencing the different types of terrain throughout the country.

One of the trips with the Hyundai was over the Rocky Mountains. That trip took us to an elevation of over 11,000 feet. In a normal, American car that would not have been a problem. With the Hyundai, we had a problem. Loaded down as we were, and with the five of us aboard, and at that elevation, that little bugger would not go over thirty-five miles per hour, and that was on the Interstate. Can you imagine how embarrassing it was for all the big rigs to be passing us as though we were standing still? I was the guy who had previously owned a '66 GTO and a '68 Dodge Charger RT, not to mention that Nisson 280ZX. Would I have ever had such a problem with those cars? Oh, hell no! How humiliating can you get?

As often as we preplanned many of the sights we wanted to see, nearly as frequently we would divert from the main road and just head out into unknown territory. On one such occasion, while travelling through northern Arizona, we ran across a Navaho station on the radio. We were listening to the Navaho language and music for a long time, and then it occurred to us we were actually very near a large Navaho reservation. We left the main road and went off in the direction of the reservation. We had no clue after a while where we were, but we saw some fascinating sights before we left the area. We wanted so badly to take some pictures, but that was strictly forbidden. If you were caught, you would be forcibly removed from the reservation at the very least. It was not worth taking the risk, at least not with my family. Besides, we also were not ready to take the risk of alienating the spirits. Who needs that while on vacation travels? As adventurous as all of us might have been, we were not related to Chevy Chase. Now and then we were actually somewhat cautious.

On another journey, while driving through New Mexico, we had heard about the famous, ancient Cliff Dwellings. We had to see them. They were nowhere near the main Interstate. We had to drive nearly a hundred miles out of our way, but we were on vacation. What else did we have to do but get back home? That time we were on our way back home to California from another Michigan trip.

We were all amazed by what we saw. How those civilizations lived up in the cliffs and carried on normal lives is a mystery. The ancient dwellings were carved into the vertical cliffs hundreds of feet above the gorge below. Had there been a sleepwalker among them, it would have resulted in a much shorter life than expected. I can certainly understand how they could have been safe from their enemies, but how difficult life must have been for them is hard to imagine.

Another trip took us the southern route, through the "great" state of Texas. It was hot and dry, and, when we spotted a river with a large recreation area, we turned immediately in that direction. A nice swim in cool, clear water sounded like a terrific idea. We stopped, put on our bathing suits and plunged into the river. The water did not really look very clean and pure, and the other people in the water did not exactly look clean and pure either. Although it was not as refreshing as we had hoped, we tried not to think about it, and just enjoyed ourselves as much as possible, which did include a water slide out in the middle of the river, along with a hundred others in the river. The decision to stop off at that river might have been just a little hasty.

The following day Deb became terribly ill. The bug hit me next, and before we got to Michigan, we all felt like we were close to death, with perhaps some exaggeration. My oldest son, Craig, and I bonded together with our heads over the toilet at my in-laws' house in Michigan. What a wonderful trip that turned out to be. A message to the wise would be to use caution when looking at the refreshing qualities of a Texas river. No offense to all my Texas friends, but the term "great" referred to above could just mean large, as the largest state in the continental US. In my humble opinion, there was nothing great about that river, and, yes, I am sure I will hear about that comment.

Another of our family adventures was once again one of our infamous family summer trips, this time not going all the way across country, but just up the coast through California, Oregon and Washington. My brother-in-law, being in the Coast Guard, was stationed at Port Angeles, Washington. We were going up to visit him and his wonderful wife, and the Fourth of July weekend seemed like a good time to do it.

We were not at all considering the fact that travelling on the Fourth of July weekend could cause us some significant problems. It was just one of the busiest weekends of the summer season. Why would we ever think we would run into problems on such a weekend? From San Diego, we made it past San Francisco, and we began to tire and look for a hotel to spend the night. We chose not to sleep in the car that night. We needed good sleep and we knew we would not get it in the car.

We must have stopped at twenty hotels, and none of them had any vacancies. We were finally so tired we could not hold it together anymore. We had to find somewhere to sleep. Finally, we spotted a rag-tag looking motel, but by that time, we could not have cared less how the place looked. We wanted a bed, immediately or sooner.

We had our wish. We had a room with two beds and a couch. It even had a small kitchen. What more could we ask? It would be just fine for the five of us. Well, the first thing we discovered was the place was absolutely filthy. The rugs were nasty, the bathroom, and the bathtub itself, had mold everywhere. The towels were nasty and the beds were so uncomfortable we hardly got any sleep at all. It was by far the worst excuse for a hotel we had ever encountered. There were even bugs running all over the place. It really gave us the creeps. We would have been much better off just staying on the road and trying to catch a few winks in the car wherever we could. That was definitely not the best travel night we had ever had, but we will never claim it was not another adventure through which the family bonded and grew. What a way to grow, right?

We never met with Deb's brother that week, as he was on duty and his boat was out of port. We did stay at his house, however. We saw some beautiful country, along with the entire coastline up to Washington. We stopped at the Monterey Aquarium and had a fantastic visit, which included losing our middle son, Brent, for an hour or so. He had a phenomenal ability to disappear in an instant, and did it on more than one occasion. Nevertheless, we observed more sea life there than most people can see in a lifetime. One of the highlights was the assortment of jellyfish in a fantastic exhibit. We were all completely fascinated with that display. It was a great day for all of us, even though it would have seemed for a while that we had one less son. We were beginning to get used to it by that time.

One of the most significant drives we took on that trip, after having explored most of the Olympic peninsula, was our visit to the top of Mount Saint Helens. That trip was four or five years after the infamous Mount Saint Helens volcanic eruption of May 18, 1980, and the total devastation that occurred on that mountain. The results of that cataclysmic eruption were still extremely visible everywhere we looked. The trees were still splintered and strewn in every direction. I have heard it described by others, and see it in photographs, as looking like toothpicks or pick-up sticks from the air. What used to be green vegetation everywhere was only mud as far as the eye could see. We saw, of course, where a third of the mountain had just disappeared. It was amazing. The explosion had caused winds of up to 300 miles per hour at a temperature over 600 degrees Fahrenheit. There were four billion board feet of lumber lost, which is enough to build 300,000 two-bedroom homes. There were fifty-seven people killed in the blast. The pyroclastic flow cleared everything in its path in just minutes. Those statistics are from a USGS report that we found at the visitor center.

When we reached the top of the mountain, the weather was as bad, or worse, than it had been the whole trip up there. It was cold, rainy, and dark by the time we arrived. We found nothing open. There were no accommodations anywhere. We were hoping to find at least a convenience store or something open where we might be able to use a bathroom or get a drink. We did find a store at the top, but it was closing as we arrived. We were as far as we wanted to go; so, we just decided to park in the lot of the store, sleep it off for the night and catch them in the morning. We did find the proprietor of the store, and he gave us permission, upon our asking, to sleep the night in our car in his parking lot, so we could see the mountain the next day.

As time passed further into the night, the wind and rain increased, our little car began to rock back and forth, and we were not getting much sleep. The storeowner had become concerned about us, and he came out to check. He carried a shotgun, but assured us we had nothing to worry about. He invited us to come into the store to warm up. He had been nervous about strangers in his parking lot at night, because he had had trouble in the past. It was obvious to him we were a family with three small boys and we could use some help. He even offered us mattresses to sleep on and hot chocolate to help warm us up. He was as nice as you could possibly imagine. We had made a new friend.

The next morning we woke up, the shop owner made us breakfast, and gave us great directions for the most interesting things to see, weather permitting. The weather was still bad as we left, and we were on our way again. We did not see as much as we would have if the weather had been better, but we saw enough to make a lasting impression on all of us. There was also a museum, which gave us the history of the mountain and the eruption details, and an explanation of exactly what happened, as well as the results and future impact. It had to have been at least one of our exposures to volcanic activity that helped to lead Craig, my oldest son, into geology and volcanology. He does have his master's degree in geology, and he spent two years working toward a PhD in lava flow patterns and geothermal energy in Australia.

On our way down the mountain, we stopped off at a few of the touristy gift shops for samples of volcanic ash and some ceramic trinkets and other gifts made from the volcanic ash from the eruption. We still have a few of those today to reinforce the memories. That was pretty much the end of that trip. We headed back to good old sunny southern California. It was another adventure none of us has ever forgotten.

Our favorite route across the US was always the northern route, just because we always loved going through all of the mountains on the way, including the great canyons of Utah, the northern Rockies, the Grand Tetons, the Black Hills of South Dakota, the Badlands and on into Yellow Stone National Park. We always made lengthy stops at the caves in the Black Hills. Jewel Cave, Wind Cave and Ice Cave were the main attractions, and we saw them all, each an adventure in itself. While in the area, we, of course, never missed Mount Rushmore, always a majestic sight to see, although becoming more and more touristy all the time. Coming out of the Black Hills, we drove into the Badlands, which again was unique. It is an awesome trip, and, of course, with three boys we always had to get out of the car and explore. It was not just the boys. We all loved it.

One of my favorite stories from the Badlands is when we were on one of our exploratory expeditions. We were in a climbing mood and stopped at one fascinating spot. We jumped out of the car and were ready to tackle the hills. There are limitations as to where tourists can walk around in the Badlands. The rangers are very protective of the area, as well as having a concern for the safety of people wandering around the dangerous slopes of those sandstone mountains. We had our eyes on the steepest and highest hill in sight, and we were more than ready for the climb.

Consisting of nearly a hundred percent sandstone, the Badlands are a bit precarious when it comes to climbing around on them. They crumble easily and are very slippery, even when dry. Of course, my bonehead family, and I do include myself, as their great, heroic leader, has climbed them even in the rain where it is more than just a little slippery. On this particular day, however, there was beautiful weather and everything was perfectly dry and as safe as one can expect. My family, somewhere along the line, developed a kind of "no fear" attitude about life in general, and I have no idea from where that might have come. I know I could never have been responsible for that attitude. I plead ignorance. Anyway, you will plainly see the following sequence was not entirely of my volition.

We progressed up the mountain in our little column of ducks, dad in the lead, the three boys, and Deb bringing up the rear. After a lengthy climb, which began with a rope ladder up a very steep slope, we began crossing a ridge with a drop of about a hundred feet on each side. We were not in any real danger until I came upon a wide break in the ridge, which in order to cross it, we would have to jump across the break about two and a half feet. The drop, should anyone not quite make the jump, would be, as I stated, somewhere close to a hundred feet, accompanied by probable death. Why would that ever stop us?

I stopped to appraise the situation a little more closely. I determined it was too dangerous to try, and decided we should turn back and find a different route. Deb was not seeing the problem from twenty feet or so behind me. She had other ideas about it. Now, generally she was the one who had always been the most cautious, particularly when it came to the boys' safety. This time it seemed to be a little different.

From the rear of the pack I heard, "What are you doing up there? Let's go!" I answered with, "I'm looking at a break in the ridge, and it looks too dangerous to go on. We need to turn around and go back." Without coming forward to take a closer look, she just retorted, "You bunch of wimps! Get going and jump across!" I answered again, "I don't think you want to do this. It really is dangerous. I think we need to turn back."

Deb, from where she was, had only a limited view of what was up ahead. All she saw was a little break requiring a short hop and moving out smartly. Part of the mountain was blocking her view, and she just saw the possibility of a minor mishap if anyone slipped, maybe some insignificant bumps or scratches. It did not occur to her there was a death-defying drop to the left.

Deb was getting just a little anxious and impatient with us and came back with, "All right, do you need me to lead the way?" Of course, I could not allow that to happen and just said, "No, I'm going, but you better follow behind us." I stepped back to gain a little momentum and took my hop across the break. No problem. Next, the three boys followed in suit. They all made it, again without incident. Then Deb stepped up to the break and looked down, and then looked back up at the four of us and said, "Oh, my gosh, are you kidding me? I can't do that."

I just looked at her. After a moment I said, "Oh yeah, you can and will do it or die trying. You insisted on our jumping across this gap, and now it's your turn. Go for it, baby." I think she really thought she was going to die on that one, but she did learn a good lesson that day. "Look (and think) before you leap," right? Possibly, we were not quite as wimpy as we might have looked. She took the giant leap, and did survive it, and even enjoys talking about it today.

CHAPTER 10 – THE BIG MOVE EAST

After Deb and I had lived in California for about fifteen years, and I had worked at my high school teaching position for over twenty years, as I previously explained, I eased out of that teaching position and decided our family was going to be closer to Deb's family. It was time to move to Michigan. That was to be our last family trip across country together, but it was not an entirely uneventful trip. I was driving a big twenty-six-foot U-Haul van, and my middle son, Brent, was travelling with me, while the rest of the family was following behind in our mini-van.

We were driving through the state of Indiana when we came into a construction area on the outskirts of Indianapolis, if I recall correctly. The road was becoming rough and the lanes of the highway were merging. I had to change into the next lane to my right. I looked carefully in both side-view mirrors, but most cautiously in the right mirror. I saw no one close to me. I signaled well in advance of my move to the right, looked again, seeing no one there, and began my change of lanes.

In a few seconds Brent, who was riding in the passenger seat, said, "Dad, I think you may have just hit someone." I had not felt a thing and said, "No, I didn't; there was nobody there, and I didn't feel anything." He came back with, "Yeah, well, I think you may have. I thought I heard and felt something." I was getting a little concerned at that point and started looking everywhere I could, at first still not seeing anyone. Then suddenly a little grey car came cruising up on my right, and five or six very angry black people were shaking their fists at me, and their faces did not appear to be those of happy campers. I also noticed the front left fender had all but disappeared, and it did seem by the looks of the car they had tangled with someone on the road recently.

Even though I was less than enthusiastic about pulling over, I knew what we had to do. I took the next exit, as there was nowhere else to pull off with road construction everywhere. I found a large parking lot to pull into, and the other car was right with me. As I got out of the truck, the occupants of the other vehicle were already out, and they were all very big (and I am not), and they had very ugly expressions on their faces. They immediately began lashing out at me, the driver saying something like, "Look at my damn car! Do you see what you did to us? You shouldn't be driving that thing. You could have killed us!"

I was very cool about it on the outside, even though inside I was very nervous, my son being only about twelve years old at the time. I was not at all sure what was going to happen next. Deb and the other two boys were in our car behind the moving van, and she told me later their car looked like a clown car the way all those huge people came out of that small car, and all they heard were f-words those people were throwing at me.

I merely said, "Sir, I apologize sincerely for what happened, but it was not because I wasn't watching for someone in the rear and on both sides. I looked very carefully before signaling I was coming over, and then did my changeover. I wasn't even aware you were behind me, let alone that I might have hit you, until my son told me he thought I had hit someone. I assure you that I am well insured, and you will be compensated for all of the damages. We can all be thankful that no one was injured through all of this."

They all began to relax and calm down, and the anger began to dissipate right away. We exchanged insurance information, I called my insurance agency on the spot, and everything came together nicely. We parted company, all in good spirits. There were some rather tense moments for a while, and the thought that I really could have killed all of them did not leave my mind for some time.

The fact is, if someone does not see the driver of a truck in front of him or her in the truck's side-view mirror, then the driver of the truck does not see him or her either. Trying to pass on the right is never a smart move if you are not completely in control of the situation, let alone in a construction zone. I did not wish to begin a debate, however, with the occupants of that vehicle. I'm thinking it might not have gone well with that approach. Brent and I considered the day a success. It's good not to kill people.

The remainder of that trip was uneventful, I am happy to say, and we cruised right into Michigan. The next mission was to settle in. There were a few obstacles to that, however. We did have a temporary "house" in which to live, as Scott and I had travelled out earlier in the summer to establish ourselves before driving out blindly.

We were a family of five, and the street was not the best spot for the family to sleep. The only "house" we were able to find available was a very small beach cottage right on Lake Huron. Because it was the end of the summer, we were able to rent it at winter rates, which were very reasonable. That was part of the good news. On the down side, we had to fit five of us into maybe four hundred square feet of space, which included a combined kitchen, dining room and living room, a bathroom and two very small bedrooms. We were all preparing to bond into a very tightly knit family unit, and we were in for a significant challenge. We were leaving a house of over 2,000 square feet of space, with a garage, and moving into a place about one-fifth the size, without a garage. There was no avoiding having to put most of our belongings into storage. Our entire household was in a large truck. We were also looking at a major organizational task.

The township of Oscoda, Michigan is not what one might think of as a megalopolis. It is a very small community, which at the time we moved here had one self-storage facility, and that one facility did not have a single unit or even a combination of units that could store all of our household goods. Looking elsewhere, the next closest town was East Tawas, and we ran into the very same problem. There appeared to be only one solution. We had to split our household goods between two locations, fifteen miles apart, and that would not include what we had with us at the cottage. That meant we were actually in three locations. Can you imagine trying to remember which things were in which location as needs increased with time? It was little short of a nightmare.

Well, there we were in our little "doll house" right on the beach! Hey, we were in a beach cottage on Lake Huron. What more could we ask for? Although it was toward the end of the summer, we still had a short time left of decent weather. Summers are generally on the short side in northern Michigan. Being on what is referred to as "the sunrise side" of Michigan, we were able to watch the sunrise every morning, as right outside the door was the beach, and the water of Lake Huron was not more than a hundred feet from our door. Being the old "beach rats" from southern California, we were right at home in this environment. It was great...in that respect.

I should back up a few weeks before progressing any further. I mentioned that Scott and I had reconned the area in the earlier part of the summer in order to establish a place for the family to live, and, of course, I was searching for new employment. During that visit, we stayed in my sister-in-law's little camping trailer. Even though my wife was born and raised all of her young life in Michigan, we all had a good deal to learn about the area and its weather, particularly my boys and I. However, the rest of Deb's side of the family proved to me that summer they were definitely not weather experts of the area, even though they seemed to indicate otherwise.

In the nineteen summers and winters I have been able to experience this state, that first year (1995) had the most bizarre weather conditions that any of my immediate family, with the possible exception of Deb, has ever seen here. One day, just a short time after Scott and I arrived, I was sitting in my mother-in-law's house, watching the Weather Channel. I noticed that up around Traverse City, about 150 miles to the northwest of us, there was a very strong storm that had formed, and it was heading southeast at a velocity of sixty miles per hour. Oscoda was right in line with that trajectory, and a little over two hours away the way I calculated. We would not escape that storm. I was not a meteorologist, but even I could see the proverbial "writing on the wall."

At almost the same moment, my sister-in-law arrived, storming through the front door, yelling, "Hey, let's go to the beach!" My mother-in-law agreed. I interrupted with, "Hold on, guys. What I'm seeing here on the Weather Channel may not be in line with that plan. There is a very big storm heading this way from Traverse City, and I don't think we really want to be out in the lake when it hits." What the hell did I know? I was just a dumb southern Californian, and I knew less than squat about Michigan weather.

The response I received was basically, "John, we have lived here for quite a few years now, and I think we know the weather pretty well. You don't have to worry; we go through this all the time. We'll be fine. Come on." I weakened, and, of course, I did not want to be the wimp who would cower away from a little rain coming in. Besides, if the storm came in while we were out in the lake, we would just leave the lake and go home. It was as simple as that. What was there to worry about? We quickly packed up and headed out to the main beach in Oscoda.

When we arrived at the beach, we immediately ran out to swim and play in the water. We had been in the water for fifteen or twenty minutes when I noticed (to the northwest, no less) clouds and lightning strikes. Wow. How amazing is that? I called everyone's attention to it, and I began making my way toward shore. Lake Huron, as most of the Great Lakes, has a very gradual drop in depth as you move out from shore, and it takes a long time to go out to swimming depth, as well as getting back into shore. Before we could get even close to the beach, the storm hit, and it hit with unimaginable fury.

You may recall the storm was travelling at sixty miles per hour, and that is without any gusting. The winds that hit us had to have been doing eighty miles per hour at least. We were almost unable to walk without being blown over, with the horizontal rain, along with beach sand, hitting like needles. We were able to get to our towels and clothes just before the severe winds and rain hit. I put my glasses on and the wind took them right off and sent them flying. I could not even go back to get them. Ironically, I actually found them in the sand the next day when I returned. That, in and of itself, was amazing.

We struggled just to get back to the car, and then came the difficulties of making it home, not being able to see more than six or eight feet in front of us. Bucking that kind of wind was a real fight to the finish with that small car feeling like it would blow over any moment. We made it back to the house and just remained there until the storm passed. A bit later, we ventured out to assess any damages that might have occurred during the storm.

The first place we went was to my sister-in-law's house. She lived in a mobile home about five miles away. Although the wind had blown the skirts off her house, everything else seemed to be in order. Her cat, however, had been outside and had been hiding under the house when the storm hit. I don't think the poor thing ever recovered completely from the trauma she underwent. The cat was just a tad skittish from that point on.

While no one ever spotted a funnel cloud during the storm, it became apparent to me as we continued our circuit about town that there must have been a tornado, or at least a down blast, that set down in more than one location. Only a block away from my sister-in-law's place, one of the mobile homes had its roof blown off completely. We went over to the local campground, called Old Orchard Park, and found many tree blow-downs, some of which had crushed boats, cars and campers (not the people, but those on wheels). That also told us something very strong had hit our area.

Although northern Michigan is notorious for unpredictable weather, 1995 was a year for all of us to remember. Not only was the summer significant with that storm and many others less severe, but also the winter certainly had weather conditions I have yet to see matched. Try to remember this is all from the perspective of an old southern Californian, who was not accustomed to any significant weather changes throughout any year.

We were still in the lake cottage as Old Man Winter approached. The temperatures began dropping rather suddenly. We all thought we were pretty well prepared for it. I had envisioned the lake beginning to freeze little bits at a time from the shoreline outward. That is not exactly what we were seeing. The ice began to build up, not from the shoreline of the lake, but rather far out in the lake, then expanding toward the shoreline. Once most of the surface water had turned to ice, the ice began to build vertically. There were ice "mountains" arising right in front of us. It began to look like arctic tundra. Every night we could hear the ice crack, shift, and screech, moving about with the wind and tide. It was a serene, even ghostly setting. Where there was a hole in the ice, you could watch the ice "volcanoes" with the water shooting up through the ice and, because of the extreme cold, freezing on the way back down.

As well as big snow events (storms), we had a good deal of "lake effect" snow that year. The snow blew in off the lake and piled up in our front yard (the beach). It was pretty crazy, but a lot of fun for our boys, for all of us in fact. The boys went out and actually burrowed into the snow, digging snow tunnels and making their own mountains. Further out, where the water usually meets the sand, it became just flat ice, and it was a great deal of fun for not only the boys, but Dad as well. With the exception of a few rough spots, it was like a big ice rink. The boys would go out and run as fast as they could and slide across the ice, not much different from ice-skating. Of course, not to be outdone by his three small children, Dad had to try it for himself. Life is full of good and bad choices, and that was not one of my better ones.

Yes, it was mandatory for Dad to go out on the ice to show the boys what he had, to show them how it's really done. I began the big preparatory run followed by the giant leap for parenthood, both feet planted firmly on the ice, ready to slide. I did slide – for about one foot. At that moment, I saw right in front of my face, and at eye level, both of my feet. I had just enough time to think (hey, I would not actually say it in front of the boys), "Shit!" before descending quickly to make direct contact between ice and posterior. I humbled myself again that day. I was in a good deal of pain, though it seemed quite funny to everyone else. I pretty much decided at that point the boys were welcome to be the experts at that activity. I was ready to call it quits.

For the four or five months we lived in the beach cottage, we spent a great deal of time looking for a larger house that would fit our needs, and one we could afford. That time did come, but it was, of course, in the dead of winter, a wonderful time in northern Michigan to move. You do recall, of course, it was not just a matter of moving everything we owned from one residence to another. We were in three separate locations, and there was a total of at least a couple of feet of snow on the ground by that time. The fun was only beginning. We loaded up our immediate belongings from the cottage and moved that to our new house, which, of course, was just a rental. We were not yet in any position to buy a new house. I had still not found a job.

After unloading our initial household goods from the cottage, it was time to go off to the two other storage facilities. We loaded up all those goods, and, as tough as it was, it did feel good to get rid of those two storage facilities and have everything together once again. We finally had a house with everything we owned under a single roof. From then on, it was an organizational task before us, not much different from most other moves, and we were definitely used to those. We felt like professional movers by that time. Deb and I had moved at least a half dozen times in our marriage by then, and we were not even close to being finished with that ongoing task.

As we moved into the new house, we not only had a house to put together, but we also had Christmas quickly approaching. With a new house in which to live, I intended to put Christmas decorations high on our priority list. Yes, the weather was a slight drawback, but would I ever let that stop me? Oh, hell no. I was a dumb-ass southern Californian, who did not have the sense of a pumpkin (or mistletoe to put it into the right season). Ignorance was bliss and I just kept on smiling. The wind was blowing the heavy snow horizontally, hitting me in the face, the temperature being just below frostbite level, as I attempted to hang lights on a twenty-five foot tree in the front yard from the top of a six-foot ladder. That was a challenge I had never faced before. It was a wonderful and educational experience. I'm sorry. Did I sound serious? A white Christmas was pretty special, however.

The most important lesson I learned from that was that under no circumstances hang Christmas lights in blizzard-like conditions. Jesus would have forgiven me for abandoning that task, even though I would not have been showing the greatest of love to my children. I am not at all convinced I would have been able to forgive myself for that one. These days I am not opposed to hanging my lights in October if we have a nice sunshiny weekend. It works so much better than stormy, December days.

It does sound like many of my ramblings are criticisms of Michigan weather, and there really are many natives in the area who do little else but complain about the weather. Actually, my family and I were intrigued by our first Michigan winter (again, Deb notwithstanding). We actually did learn to love most of it. We had experiences that would have been impossible in most parts of the country. Granted, much of what we did was really stupid, but entertaining nevertheless.

Some of our winter madness with our children was quite dangerous, and, as parents, we might once again have been arrested today, if we were guilty of such things. Just one example was picking the boys up from their school bus stop with my pick-up truck, allowing them to hold on to the tailgate as I drove up the slick, icy road two blocks to our house. They had a great time, loving every second of it. All right, maybe I could have caused some minor injuries, but that never happened.

Apparently, Jesus does love the little children. He obviously protected them from their father.

As I already indicated, when we first moved to Michigan, I was in a job search. My area of expertise was German and English high school teaching, as well as having an extensive military background. Well, I was not pursuing the latter; so, the former was my focus. There was a bit of a problem with that, however. On my early summer trip to Michigan before our move, one of the items of business I had to take care of was my State of Michigan teaching certification.

There was a time, just a few years before our coming to Michigan, when a California teacher was able to transfer to Michigan and receive certification without being tested. The only requirement was an application. Just a year or so before we decided to move, however, the State changed its policy and required each applying teacher to be tested in the areas of his or her major and minor. I went through the process and the testing that summer, and I passed everything successfully. I was almost surprised because I had not prepared in any way for those tests, and it had been over twenty years since I had had any instruction in those areas.

I was good to go on everything, but, even after paying out several hundred dollars to accomplish that requirement, there still seemed to be a major obstacle. All over the country, money was getting tight and programs were deleted right and left. German language

The Big Move East | 241

instruction just happened to fall into that category. The German programs had already begun to die out in California, and Michigan was no different.

My last dozen years of teaching in California were all English, with most of the German programs gone by that time. There were very few remaining in Michigan when I arrived. What that meant was I was looking for a full-time high school English position. There was also a problem with that. Any school looking for a new English teacher wanted someone with a major in English, not a minor. It made no difference that I had taught the subject for twenty years. Without a major in English, I had no chance of procuring an English teaching position.

I did not let all of those obstacles deter me. I sent out well over a hundred resumes throughout the State of Michigan. I did not stop at the high schools. I reached out to the penal system, thinking that with my military background I might well stand an excellent chance at teaching at one of the state prisons. It seemed to work. I lined up three interviews at state prison facilities. After each interview, and all of them seemed to go well, the institutions informed me they were not interested in me. I could not believe what I was hearing.

After the last rejection, I called the prison to find out what was wrong with my interview or what they could tell me about my not being considered for a position. All they told me was it was against policy to divulge any information concerning interview results. I asked them how in the world I could ever hope to improve on an interview if they could not tell me what I was doing wrong. They were not at all sympathetic. It really did not matter to them.

I discovered much later it was nothing I was doing wrong. I was just not the best qualified for those positions because I would be teaching over the heads of most of my students. Most inmates are somewhere around fourth grade level, and what the prisons really needed were elementary teachers to teach high school. It finally did make more sense to me, and in retrospect, I am thankful for those rejections. I know much more now than I did then about the environments of those prisons, particularly the maximum security facilities, and I really don't think I would ever have found anything resembling enjoyment or fulfillment.

While all those interviews were going on and the resumes going out, I was still looking for just about any employment. I was not eligible for unemployment, as I had not yet had a job in Michigan. When I left the school system in California, I had little choice but to take my retirement in lump sum form, which meant, of course, I would have nothing left for the future if I needed to spend it. Having no job waiting for me in Michigan, I had to have it as back up, and, yes, I did need it and I did spend it, or what was left of it after the State of California and the IRS got their portions. That was truly a killer, and, of course, today I have nothing left of that would-be teaching retirement. Thank goodness for the military retirement. What can I say? Things always work out for the best.

Chapter 11 – Michigan Employment and Opening Stores

In the process of looking for employment, my family was attending a local church in town, and we became friends with several people. One of them happened to own the business machine dealership in Oscoda. It serviced an area of about a hundred miles in three directions. The fourth direction was Lake Huron. He needed a new sales representative and offered me the job. It paid very little, but it was a job and I was not in a position to negotiate. Because he knew we were a family of five on such a small salary, and because he and his wife were very giving people, he offered one of his unoccupied rental homes to us rent free. He said we could move into it at any time, but there were no guarantees about how long it might be available to us. We had to make a few repairs, but that was it. We could hardly believe that offer and we graciously accepted.

I continued to sell copy machines and cash registers for about three years, and Deb was going to school, working toward a bachelor's degree and teacher certification. We needed to maintain at least one teacher in the family. After about three years selling business machines we had become a little tired of having so little cash available most of the time, and I was continuing to search for more meaningful employment, perhaps something a bit more lucrative and a little closer to something for which I had been educated. Well, that was a little tough in a small town like Oscoda. A position did come up that had me working for the county health department and working with high school kids. I really thought I would enjoy that, but it became quite political, and they told me after just a few weeks they did not like my approach to guiding those young people. Well, that was short lived. They fired me.

Shortly after that little setback, a position arose for radio advertisement sales. By that time, I was a veteran salesperson. The sales profession is not always the most financially rewarding employment, but again it was another of those offers I could not turn down. I took it. Actually, before I was through with that business, I worked for two different radio stations, not only selling advertising, but actually cutting advertisements on the air and operating the station at night, monitoring the Detroit Red Wing hockey games and making local station identification add-ins. It was a fun business, and I made some nice contacts.

One day, as I was driving along US 23, the major roadway through the area, I passed the local Schwan's Ice Cream and frozen foods distributor and warehouse. Something made me stop in to inquire. Sure enough, the manager was looking for another driver. All I had to do was procure a commercial driver's license. I did that and I had a job. It was a higher paying job than the radio sales. It actually turned out to be very enjoyable employment for the most part.

I did meet some very interesting people during my employment with Schwan's, since I ended up going into the homes of every type of family imaginable. I serviced the very wealthy, as well as the very poor. I found that, expensive as the products were, our company accepted food stamps, and many people were very reluctant to buy until I called that fact to their attention. Then my sales increased remarkably.

A few of the requirements of that job were anything but desirable. Some of the homes I walked into, especially some of the mobile homes, I immediately wanted to walk right back out of. The stench frequently came close to knocking me over. For the life of me, I could not understand how anyone could allow his or her house to get to the point of smelling so bad. Sometimes it was body odor, sometimes it was animal odor, and sometimes it was just general filth. In any case, I would rather have just given up the business than to put up with those conditions. I toughed it out, however, held my breath as long as I could, and quite literally kept on "truckin'."

You may have heard about, read about or seen programs on television about people who hoard. In my Schwan's route, I confirmed that disease, or disorder, on more than one occasion. There was one home in particular, occupied by an elderly, single woman, which was so cluttered with junk you could not find your way through it. It reminded me of a maze in a laboratory through which mice run, but the walls of the junk maze went nearly to the ceiling. There were many stacks of books, but much of it was just junk, with which the woman could not part. There was no way she could throw anything away. Everything was important enough to hang onto forever.

Another unpleasant situation occurred on my Schwan's routes, primarily in the winter season, and in Michigan that season is often entirely too long. That situation dealt with pets. All pets have their needs to get out of the house and take care of their natural business. I never directed my complaints toward the pets, but rather the pet owners. Many of those people never cleaned up after their pets, and what they, mostly dogs and cats, left behind was disgusting. Rather than nice, beautiful, white, freshly fallen snow, it was yellow and brown with nasty chunks. It never made for an outstanding day, particularly if it was at night that I found that mess, and it ended up on my shoes. Yuk!

On the subject of winter and my Schwan's job, I often found myself in hazardous environments, as well as those that were just emotionally painful. An example of the latter occurred as I was driving through one of my most distant routes in the Houghton Lake area (central Michigan). I drove a very large truck from which I delivered mostly frozen foods and ice cream to my customers. As I rounded a corner, one of the doors on the driver side of the truck swung open, and at least thirty or forty half-gallons of ice cream slid out of the truck and into the street. Set the mental picture for yourself here. Envision the scene in Roger Rabbit, presuming you saw it, where he has about a hundred knives coming at him all at the same time. It was very similar to that but with ice cream cartons that were flying away from me.

I might not have even noticed had I not glanced into my side-view mirror while negotiating the corner, and seen the goods hitting the street. It was a good thing it was in the winter, as very little of the packaging was actually damaged. The street was mostly snow and ice. It also did not have a chance to melt. The truly amazing thing was how many people came to my rescue that day, coming from every direction to help. It was like a community project. I had a renewed faith in human nature that day.

A hazardous situation arose on a day I was taking someone else's route as a substitute driver. The weather took a bad turn that day, and I found myself right in the middle of a huge snowstorm. There were near whiteout conditions, making it extremely difficult to see more than twenty or thirty feet to the front. I was in an area with which I was not at all familiar. I found the house I was looking for and pulled to the right side of the road as far as I thought was safe, and yet far enough over that I would not be obstructing traffic. It appeared I still had several feet of solid ground to the right of my truck, but the depth of the snow made that very deceiving. In reality, I had something less than zero feet of solid ground. What I was seeing was snow and less than solid ice. On the other side of that illusion was a ditch that dropped fifteen or twenty feet.

Before I had even stopped to get out of the truck, I could feel the bottom falling out and the truck beginning to slip to the right. I felt complete helplessness as I attempted to accelerate and turn to the left to get my truck back up onto the road. It was not working. I was slipping further off the road. I changed strategies and tried backing up. The result was the same. I was at the point where I was ready to bail out, as I knew the truck was on its way over the edge, and I did not really want to "go down with my ship."

The truck was at about a twenty-degree angle, going over the embankment, when I decided it was most prudent to "abandon ship." I set the brake, turned off the engine and slowly and carefully climbed out the driver-side door. The truck was remaining stationary for the moment, although precariously hanging on the edge of the cliff. I climbed down and reached safety, and then called a heavy-duty towing service. The tow truck showed up in a reasonably short time, and the driver sized up the situation and came up with a plan.

The driver hooked onto my truck, took up the slack in the chain and began to pull. My Schwan's truck did not appear to have a chance. It was at such an angle that I was sure that it was going to overturn. I could see disaster ready to happen. Surprisingly it slowly came forward and out toward the street. It was a meticulous operation, done with precision, and I for one was impressed. Eventually, the truck was back on the road and we had avoided a terrible mess. The tow-truck driver was my hero for the day. I would have had a tough time explaining my way out of that situation, even though my boss was a very understanding guy. He had a good laugh about it when I explained the reason for the towing bill.

All seemed to go well with that job until my kind, understanding boss and depot manager, decided to change the rules of his business. I had hired on with the understanding I would have eight routes, one each day, four days per week and one day each week of prospecting, whereby I would go out knocking on doors to find new customers. That meant each route would have a two-week rotation. I was paid five days per week.

Then came the kicker when my manager decided we would be on our own for prospecting, because we were building our own routes, which meant we, as drivers, were generating more income for ourselves, and, therefore, the company should not have to pay for that, regardless whether or not the company was also making money on the deal. I was not pleased with that decision because it resulted in a $120.00 per week cut in my salary. That was significant enough to make me look around for other things to do, plus the fact that my routes were so long and so far away from the depot I did not get home from work until way after midnight most of the time.

The next opportunity I took advantage of was a long-term, substitute teaching position for the entire school year. By that time, my wife had acquired her degree and teaching certification, and had a permanent teaching position right in our own Oscoda Area Schools. My long-term substitute position paid me what it would have paid a full-time teacher, and that is very unusual. This meant we had two full-time teaching salaries for the year. That was to be our best year financially up to that point, and it allowed us to buy our own home after that year. The subbing position I had was seventh and eighth grade English, and that age group had never been my preference. It was a tough year, but it worked out well. It was also more than an hour travel each way to and from that school, and that was a bit time-consuming, as well as expensive. I was pleased when it was over.

Before the end of that teaching year, my friend, John, who had worked over ten years as a manager for a major discount store chain, and had changed over to store development, told me what he was up to. I had asked a few questions, and he explained he went all over the country building new stores, renovating old ones and tearing down those that were not successful. I told him that sounded very interesting. Coincidentally, he was looking for an assistant to travel with him, and he asked me if I was interested in going out on a job with him to see if it would be good for me. I agreed to it, just as soon as I was finished with the academic year, only a couple of weeks away. I went on a two-week job with him and ended up staying with the company for another five and a half years.

I could tell by that first two-week job, and that was typical of most of the jobs, I had a long way to go to learn as much as I needed to know about putting a new store together. I had a good mentor, however, as well as a good friend to guide me. As a beginning assistant, I rode with John in his company truck. A store opener was authorized a truck, but an assistant was not. Everywhere John went I went. We became the Big and Little John team, as he was nearly twice my weight, even though we looked eye to eye with one another. I actually only stayed with John as his assistant for maybe a year and a half, but we were together long enough to share many very interesting, as well as humorous, experiences.

Because we had the opportunity to travel all over the country, we worked with people in all walks of life. I went as far west as Salt Lake City, Utah, as far north as the Upper Peninsula of Michigan, and as far south as Tampa, Florida, as well as all over the eastern seaboard. For better or for worse I spent a great deal of time in the New York City area. The most significant aspect of all that travel was observing and experiencing the vast diversity of cultures all around the country. I worked with a different group of people every two weeks. It took us approximately ten days to build a new store, two days of travel, a couple of days home, and off the following Monday on a new job. It was a steady routine unless we had a different kind of project going, which was frequently the case.

Just to show some contrasts of the groups of people with whom we worked, I'll make a quick comparison of two areas. When we went to a job site, the first thing we did was contact the district manager to see if he or she had laid on temporary employees (temps) who could be there to assist us, particularly with the heavy work, like unloading fixture and merchandise trucks, as well as setting up the fixtures in the store. By store fixtures, I am referring to all the shelving, checkouts, display racks and electronics required for each store. There was also the unloading of merchandise trucks after everything else was completed.

It is tough work, and usually we hired fifteen to twenty temps for each store, and we often took them right off the street. Store openers and assistant openers were there to direct and supervise the activities. By no means did that mean we did not get right into the action and get our hands dirty. It often got very physical and very dirty, downright nasty, particularly on store closings and renovations. John often told me to stop doing the dirty work and let a temp take care of it. More often than not, it was just not convenient to do that. It was easier and faster to do it myself. Often I would not allow a temporary employee to do some of the dangerous things I did. It was very often a bad idea for me to do it. I frequently ran into trouble when I did.

One particularly nice job we had was in Chili, New York (and we were told the town's name was never pronounced chili, as in chili sauce – it was with two long i's). Chili is a college town, and, as such, the local people looking for work were mostly college kids. Nearly the entire crew we hired was composed of college students, and they were probably the smartest group I ever worked with.

Most of the time the caliber of people we had to hire, for the low wages we had to pay, was quite low. Most temps were people who were unemployed much more frequently than they were employed, and their intelligence levels were quite low. When teaching these folks how to do a task, like counting spaces between shelves, it often takes five or six tries before they get it right. With that Chili group, you could tell them once and they had the whole concept all together. They could have become supervisors after doing each task once. That was it, and we hardly ever had to look to see if they had done it right. That was a given. It was among the easiest jobs we ever had.

We had many jobs with the opposite situation, whereby our people were so brain dead they could hardly function. Those jobs were the hardest to accomplish. If our temps could not handle certain jobs, we would have to do it ourselves. It was not often we had to tell someone to hit the road, but now and then, it did happen. If they came in under the influence of drugs or alcohol, we had to tell them to keep on going. We had no tolerance for that, even though we were only paying minimum wages. If they showed us an attitude or refused to abide by our rules, then we would warn them once, and then ask them not to return. The system worked well. Most groups were very good and got the job done well and on time.

Whether our work projects were good or bad, there were incidents that made the individual jobs very memorable. Many of those projects were with my old friend, John. I frequently found myself at the top of a ten-foot ladder in the middle of a store. He did also, but, because he was nearly twice my weight, though considerably younger, I generally volunteered to go up into the ceilings. Most of the time the reason I was at ceiling level was to install wiring for the cash registers or other electronics.

There was one time I was doing exactly that, when my ladder suddenly went south, or it may have been west, but it was no longer under my feet, which was not good news. I was hanging onto one of the rafters with my feet dangling below. At first, I was quite calm and tried to get John's attention without screaming bloody murder. I merely called out to him, "John, could you come over here for a moment? I've got a problem." He was busy at something and definitely not paying any attention to what I was doing. He said, "Yeah, I'll be there in a minute," not looking up from his work.

I waited for a few moments and he still was not coming to my rescue.

I tried once again, "John, I really do need you over here. Can you break off from what you're doing for a moment?"

He still failed to look up and just said, "Man, I said I'll be there in a minute."

At that point, because I was ready to fall ten feet straight into the cash registers below me, I lost just a bit of my composure and yelled, "John, get your ass over here now!"

He then looked up from his work and saw my rather precarious position. "Oh, crap! I'm sorry. Why didn't you say something?" he cried out, as he scrambled across the floor to where I was, and put the ladder back under me. I calmly, but perhaps a bit sarcastically, thanked him for rescuing me.

Speaking of ladders, there was also the time I was working in the same environment, again up on a ten-foot ladder. In that case I was just too short, even standing on the very top of that ten-footer, which even the warnings on the ladders tell you not to do, to reach up to make the electrical connection. Normally I would have asked one of our taller temps to get up on the ladder to help, but on that job, all of the taller people were acrophobic. The mere thought of climbing up a ten-foot ladder scared them silly. I did not want them up there. So, while up in the ceiling on my tiptoes and, about four inches short of my goal, I grabbed a steel beam and pulled myself up far enough to make the connection. My mission was successful and all I had to do was lower myself back to the ladder below me. I came down, and my foot hit the ladder with all of my weight at the same time, and I lost my grip from above. The ladder took off, and this time I went with it.

There were actually several things going through my mind at that moment. The first was a simple, very brief "Oh crap!" The second thought was, "Where did I put that little, three-foot section of shelving I just built? Is it right where I am about to hit? Am I really going to hit that shelf section and break myself in half?" I had just enough time left in my fall for one more thought, and that was, "Thank you, Lord, for my airborne training. I think I can make a successful landing here, as long as I don't hit anything on the way down." It was indeed a long way down, but I really did manage to make a great PLF (parachute landing fall) on a nice clear tile floor.

Those who witnessed the fall were reasonably sure I would be either dead or on my way to the hospital. Fortunately, neither was the case. I got up a little shaky, but everything was still working and unbroken. I brushed myself off and was ready to go back up the ladder to replace the ceiling tile. I finished everything I had to do up there. There were quite a few disbelieving head-shakers afterward. Yes, my good old guardian angels were still on the job. I never have given them much rest. They will all probably be happy to see me finally just die. I would rather not give them that much satisfaction too early, however.

I really can't help but chuckle when I think about the job I was on with another store opener, Andy, for whom I was an assistant. Now and then, his wife would come along with him on a job, and she would put in a good deal of work, as she did have prior experience with this business. Health forced her to stop doing it on a regular basis. That job was a store closure, as opposed to building a new store. We had already torn the store down, cleaned it up well, and were ready to move the saved fixtures onto one of our big, contract trucks, parked outside the store.

The store was actually part of a shopping center, and there was a sidewalk just outside the front door, which slanted as you exited to the right. It was a slight downhill grade to get to the fixture truck. My proven way of stacking shelves onto a pallet was to stack three shelves one way, then three at a ninety-degree angle, and continue to alternate until the stack was eight to ten shelves high. Then we would move the pallet with a pallet jack to the truck and unload it.

Andy insisted I stack the shelves his way, which was to have all shelves facing the same direction. I told him it would not work. We had to roll the pallet jack over a large bump going out the door, and then down a ramp (sidewalk). The shelves would shift if they were not alternated. He insisted. He was my boss and he knew everything.

Andy's wife, Terri, was helping me move the pallet jack, stacked with shelves, toward the door. As she steadied the shelves, I pulled the pallet jack toward the door. I had to pull it over the bump across the doorway in order to get it outside. The stack of shelves began to shift. I told her to push on one side of the stack to even up and balance the shelves. She did, and it improved the situation, but I was still more than a little leery of making it all the way.

We made it out the door and were beginning to move down the sidewalk, when, after two more feet forward, the shelves began shifting again. Regrettably, I was on the downhill side of the pallet jack, the direction the shelves were sliding. It would have been much worse, however, if Terri had been in that spot. Terri lost control, and the shelves were suddenly coming at me like an avalanche, so quickly I had no time to think, let alone move in the right direction. Where I should have moved to the right or left, I decided to try to outrun that onslaught. That was a very bad decision. The stack of shelves hit me first right in the back of my ankles, knocking my feet out from under me. I landed on my back on top of the shelves, which were still sliding down the sidewalk. It was a sight that should have been recorded on video. I was in a great deal of pain, but it was unbelievably funny at the same time. It probably would have made one of the best of America's Funniest Videos. That one, once again, did leave a few marks.

One of the worst jobs I ever had there was a store renovation in West Haven, Connecticut, not because the job itself was particularly difficult, but because of the events that occurred during the course of it. It was actually a simple job, which only took maybe five days to accomplish. It was the second or third day of the job and I was working on something, when my boss (Andy's boss also) called me to discuss where I was to go after this job. I had to pull out my wallet and my calendar to check the dates and write down all of the information.

While I was still trying to take care of that business, one of the temps was having a problem with which he needed my help. I left my wallet on an end cap where I was working while I helped the temp. When I returned, although it took a while to get back to what I was doing, I discovered my wallet was not where I left it. The store never closed while we were working there. Business was as usual with customers coming and going all the time we worked. A customer had stolen my wallet.

I had about $260.00 in the wallet, and that did hurt, but my major concern was that in a little over a week, I was going to have to fly to New York City from Michigan, and I now had no picture identification and no credit cards. That would not make for easy travel. My good fortune was I was retired military, and about six months before I had been issued a new military identification card, and I figured the information would still be fresh on the computers at a military installation. New London was just about an hour up the road (I-95) and that was the location of the Coast Guard Academy, as well as the New London Submarine Base.

I contacted the sub base and told them about my situation and that I needed a new military ID. They were very cooperative and told me to come right up and they would take care of me. Knowing I was on my way, they let me on base without any identification, and what I needed was right at the front gate. They had a computer and an ID section where they made me a new card on the spot in about ten minutes. I was grateful to them for that. I decided then that maybe I should not give the Navy such a tough time anymore. You have no idea how hard that is for me. I love the old interservice rivalry.

I headed back to the store, and Andy and I continued work for the next two or three days. Upon finishing that store, we headed in opposite directions. He actually had something of an emergency at home, and I told him to leave a little early and I would finish the West Haven store by myself. We were nearly finished except for cleaning up and packing up our equipment, including my pallet jack. I had acquired my own truck by that time, and Andy, of course, had his own with him; so, there was no transportation problem at all.

The day after Andy left, I went into the store early in the morning to finish up, and I had one of the regular store employees working with me. We had finished most of our work by about 10:30 A.M. and the two of us were loading my pallet jack into my truck. We both grabbed it by the bottom and lifted it up to the tailgate. He was considerably taller than I was, and I did not feel like I was holding it with my hand in the right position. I said, "Hang on a minute. I need to reposition my right hand." Just as I said that, the handle of the pallet jack came my way, and I felt a significant pinch and pain in my right pinky finger. I yelled out, "Ouch, it got me. Put it back down." We lowered the pallet jack to the ground, and I brought my hand up to look at it, thinking I had been pretty badly pinched. Nearly half of my right pinky had disappeared. Wow, that startled me. My comment was, "Oh, crap!" I seem to say that quite a lot. I looked down, and right next to my foot was my finger. "Oh, crap." I couldn't think of anything more appropriate to say. I had lost something even more important than my wallet.

As I was standing there looking at my bloody stub, I looked over at my employee and said, "Uh, would you mind going into the store and finding me a paper towel? I think I may have a leaker here." He jumped right on it and apparently told someone in the store what had happened, and the manager called 911. It was only a short time before an emergency vehicle showed up with paramedics. They gave me a personal invitation to accompany them to the hospital.

I probably looked silly, but I had picked up my finger and was carrying it around for probably over an hour. Finally, one of the paramedics said something to me about it and suggested I might put it on ice in a plastic bag. I agreed it might be a good idea, not just to preserve it better, but I might be freaking people out who might be watching me carrying a dead finger around with me.

The doctor at the hospital wanted to go ahead and do the surgery right away, but I talked them into waiting until the next morning, because I still had some work to do at the store just to finish up. They patched my finger and I went back to the store to put the final touches on everything. It took me another five or six hours and then the store was complete. I rested up in my hotel room that night and reported into the hospital the next morning. They took care of the necessary surgery and I was again on my way to the next job. After that job, I returned home to Michigan for the weekend. I never took a day off, except for the drive to my next job. How's that for job loyalty? No, it wasn't for the extra hours; I was on salary.

The evening of the accident, I made a few calls from my hotel, one of which was to my wife to explain what had happened that day. She really was very concerned about me and sympathetic with what had happened. In all of her sensitivity, she brought to my attention one aspect of my accident I might not have thought of. She told me I might very well have a tough time with the keyboard of my computer, missing that pinky. I told her how much I appreciated all of the heart-felt thoughts and outpouring of love I was then feeling.

I found out later Deb was absolutely right. That right finger, what's left of it, really does not do the trick anymore. Now and then, I actually do hit a key with that stub, but seldom, and it's not necessarily the right key. I have learned to type with nine fingers. I also have difficulty finding a pair of gloves with a short right pinky. My right gloves look funny now, one glove finger filled with nothing but air. Hey, I could have lost the whole thing. I'm thankful for what's left... or is that right?

The night after the surgery to amputate the finger, I called home to get a little sympathy, since I was not feeling great. What I received was, "What do you expect? You lost a finger, and didn't even take any time off!" I couldn't argue with that, but, hey, I was a busy man.

There is another plus to missing that finger. Being a substitute teacher, I do have fun with kids in the classroom. In the lower grades, I am known as the sub with a stub. Kids are fascinated looking at that finger, particularly when I tell them the story of how it happened. It is really fun to watch them react. Some are completely fascinated and just stare in amazement. Some look terribly concerned about the whole thing, and then there are those who need to know how it happened and how much it must have hurt. They are very surprised when I tell them how much it did not hurt.

Finally, there is one more good result of that loss; I gained a new bed. The insurance did come through; not as much as I might have hoped for, but enough to buy a big, beautiful, new, king-sized bed we would not have been able to afford otherwise. Ah, yes, the wonders of it all: the silver lining seems to remain with the cloud all the time. Deb loves our bed so much she is not convinced that I should not figure out how to lose another finger. I would rather sell a few thousand books instead.

One of the most interesting aspects of my store chain position was just the travel involved getting to some of those job sites. In the beginning, I went with John as his assistant and, of course, in his truck. Later I had my own truck and went off to join other openers as an assistant for them. Frequently, if the job were a very long distance from my home, I would drive my truck to a nearby airport, leave it parked there and fly to the city of the job site.

It was on one of my earlier jobs with the company that I went with John and we did drive all the way to New York City to do a new store. It was the latter part of August of 2001. The only hotel we could find that was within our price range was, I believe, a Holiday Inn Express, which was located right across the street from the Newark, New Jersey airport. Every day on the way to our job site in New York, we headed down the expressway with the Twin Towers right in front of us. They stood there majestically just as clear as could be.

Less than two weeks after we left that job the Twin Towers were gone. The airport right across the street from where we were staying was the origin of the flight that went down in Pennsylvania on September 9, 2001. We had been so close in time and distance to that infamous 9/11 cataclysm it left us with chills when it did happen. We had just been there days before. Our timing could have been so much worse. We were thankful for that. It was just another near miss.

It was very interesting the way I actually inherited my first company truck. Being an assistant store opener, I was not authorized my own truck, as those were only for the regular openers. I mentioned earlier I was perfectly content remaining an assistant, and had requested never to be promoted to store opener. I considered myself, for the most part, retired, and I was not intending to begin a new career. At the time I began working with that store chain, I was, I believe, fifty-seven years old.

While I was on a job in southwestern Michigan, we had several visiting openers with us on the job, and one of them I had met before, when he was the manager of the biggest store in the country at the time, which was in Detroit. We'll just call him Richard. He was a very young man, still in his mid-twenties, I think, and had been struggling considerably at the job. When it ultimately became too much for him to handle, he left management and went into store development as a store opener.

Richard had been raised in Detroit all of his young life and never lived anywhere else. That should mean he knew the town extremely well in every way. One day, while Richard was driving his company truck through that ever-so familiar town, he spotted a beautiful young "lady" standing on a street corner, and proceeded to stop to talk to her. Anyone with any brains at all, most particularly someone who had lived in that town all his life, would know that in the city of Detroit a woman standing alone on a corner, scantily dressed, is probably a prostitute, and, if she is really beautiful, she is probably an undercover police officer. However, our friend, Richard, was apparently not able to figure that one out. He was not quite as smart as many took him to be. He picked her up (in his company truck) and she subsequently arrested him. Yes, she was indeed a cop.

It was one thing to do something stupid like that in the first place, but doing it with a company truck was insane, particularly if Richard had been interested in establishing a career with the company. A few days into that job, a couple of our higher-ranking supervisors came into the store and invited "Poor Richard" back to the store office for a consultation. When they reemerged, my boss informed me I would be taking him home to Detroit, personally delivering him to his house, and retaining his vehicle.

Michigan Employment and Opening Stores | 269

From that point on, I had my own truck. It was bad news for the perpetrator of the crime, but good news for me. I was one of the few assistant openers in the company who had his own truck. There was talk that I would have to give it up, but that never happened. I was much happier in my job after that, since I had much more flexibility. The company had always paid for my hotels and food, and now they paid for all the gas expenses and repairs for the truck they had given me. It also meant I did not have to buy another new car for myself. Life was good.

As I previously indicated, if the job were a good distance away, which was frequently the case, and there were to be other openers on location with their own company trucks, I would be required to drive to an airport, put my vehicle in long-term parking and fly to wherever I had to go. It was presumably cheaper that way. Most of the time there were few, if any, problems. Occasionally, however, some things came up which caused some tension with the travel itinerary. After 9/11, there were always a few more difficulties, primarily with airport security, than before that time. I had one travel day where just about everything imaginable happened that could make for a very bad day. My flight was leaving from Detroit and my final destination was to be Greenville, South Carolina.

My flight was to depart from Detroit, which was a good four-hour drive from where I live. I had no idea beforehand, but President Bush was also coming to town that same day. It was, of course, post 9/11; so, security was tight enough anyway, even without the arrival of the President. I checked my bags at the ticket counter and was ready to go through security.

After my carry-on bag and briefcase had gone through the screening, I was facing two airport security guards. One of them asked me if I minded their looking through my briefcase. I said, "Not in the slightest. Go right ahead." As they were looking through the bag, one of them came up with a box opener, and it was the kind with an extending blade of about three inches. I used that kind for cutting holes in ceiling tiles for electrical connections. I really had no idea I had box openers in my case. I had purchased them earlier and had completely forgotten to check my bag before going to the airport. That was another "Whoops!"

The security agent held it in front of him, extended the blade, stared at it for a moment, stared at me for a moment and back to the blade. Then he and his buddy looked at each other for a couple of seconds. Right after the security guard rolled his eyes back, I said, "I'm thinking that I'm in a hell of a lot of trouble right now, right?"

With a subtle nod of his head, as well as a look of disgust, he said, "Uhh, yeah."

Well, to make a long story a little shorter, they were actually very nice about it, even though they detained me for about forty-five minutes. They actually escorted me back to baggage check to deposit those box openers into my luggage, which had not yet gone out to the plane. Actually, I had more than one. I had five of them! I could not believe they even let me keep them. Fortunately, I had arrived at the airport very early that day and did not miss my flight, even with of all that. While I was detained, they had run a criminal check on me, and, if it had not come out perfectly clean, I would have gone off to jail. They did assure me of that. Sounds like a bad day, right? The day was not over by a long shot. Stay tuned.

Because the flight was going into North Carolina, there was no way to avoid going into Charlotte. Every flight within 500 miles of Charlotte has to stop there for some reason. As we approached Charlotte, I heard an announcement over the loudspeaker that this same aircraft, after a brief stop in Charlotte, would continue on to Greenville. I stopped the flight attendant, as she passed, to confirm what I thought I heard. I said, "Excuse me, but I thought I heard that this aircraft is continuing on to Greenville. Is that correct?"

She said, "Yes."

"So," I continued, "If this aircraft is going on into Greenville, and that is my destination, I shouldn't have to get off the plane at all in Charlotte, right?"

She said, "No, I don't suppose you do have to get off." That was simple enough. I would just stay aboard and be off to Greenville upon our next departure.

After a half hour or so on the ground, all passengers boarded the plane, and in a few moments, we were in the air again. Upon landing, all passengers deplaned and we all went off to baggage claim. Long after all the other passengers had claimed their bags, it occurred to me mine had not arrived. That is not terribly unusual. I have arrived without my baggage before. I went over to the baggage claims office and questioned them. I said, perhaps being just a tad sarcastic, "Wouldn't it seem logical to you that, if I were coming from Detroit to Greenville that my luggage should also arrive in Greenville?"

She looked at me with a rather blank stare and responded, "Yes, it would seem very logical if that were the case. However, you are not in Greenville. You are in Greensboro."

"Greensboro? How far am I from Greenville?"

"About three and a half hours."

"By plane?"

"No, by car."

"I'm flying. I have no car."

"Then go upstairs to the ticket counter and buy a new ticket. You'll have to go through Charlotte though."

"Oh, crap. I'm already late for my pick-up in Greenville."

"Sir, you need to go upstairs. I cannot help you at all."

"I know that. Thank you anyway."

With that, it was off to the ticket counter. I showed them my ticket and told them I needed to get to Greenville as soon as possible. They told me there was a flight out to Charlotte (Wow, really?) in about an hour and I could catch a connection to Greenville from there. Waiting in the terminal for my next flight, I was seated in front of two doors. One led to the aircraft bound for Greenville and the other led to an aircraft, I believe, going to Chattanooga, Tennessee. Both flights were leaving at the same time.

The announcement came for the Greenville flight to board. I went to the door from which I understood my flight was leaving. Both of these planes were just small commuter, prop-driven airplanes. I took my seat, the engines started up, and the door closed. Shortly after the door closed, it opened again, and a male agent came back through the door and asked, "Is there anyone on this flight going to Greenville, South Carolina?"

I sheepishly raised my hand and asked, "Aren't we all?"

He gave me the old Cheshire cat grin and said, "No, sir, would you come with me, please?"

I got out of my seat and he escorted me over to the other aircraft. That would only have been two wrong flights for one day if they had not caught it. As it was, I was arriving nearly five hours later than the original schedule had me coming into Greenville. Isn't air travel a wonderful convenience? Then again, it may not be the best means of transportation for those who are half-deaf either.

I don't really want to go on forever about all my little incidents associated with my adventures with that company, but I would definitely be remiss if I were to leave out my little encounter in NYC with a New York City cop, which was a head-on collision. It was not quite as bad as it may sound, and yet it was no picnic either.

I was on my way to a job site one morning when it occurred to me that I was actually driving in the wrong direction for where I needed to be going. Fortunately, I was not in a terribly congested downtown area; it was a more rural section, but there was still very heavy traffic. I looked for a left-turn lane, in order to go around the block and get back to where I came from.

I finally found one, but sure enough, there was a semi approaching from the opposite direction, and wanting to make a left turn also, in the opposite direction of my intended turn. My view of on-coming traffic was partially obscured by the truck while he was waiting to make his turn. I could see back to the end of his truck and there were several cars that would be coming up on the right side of the truck to pass him. I waited for all of them to come by, and I could see no more of them.

When it seemed there were no more vehicles coming, I slowly inched into my turn, carefully watching to make sure that there were no more vehicles coming from behind or alongside of the truck. I saw nothing until a car whizzed out of nowhere and slammed so hard into the front of my truck that my truck flipped around a hundred and eighty degrees, whereby I was now facing in the opposite direction. He hit with such impact both of our air bags deployed, and, in order to get out of my truck, I had to push on the driver-side door with my feet to get it open, and he was only driving a very small compact car. It was a thirty-five mile per hour speed zone, but he had to have been doing at least fifty-five when he hit me.

I was perfectly all right except where the air bag had hit me in the face. My first concern was how the other driver fared. When I finally got out of my truck, I went back to his vehicle to see how he was. He claimed he was perfectly all right also. I saw red marks on his face also from the air bag in his own vehicle. We came out in about the same condition.

He got out of his vehicle and walked around, as though there were nothing at all wrong with him physically, and I was again relieved. While he was wandering around, I also noticed and heard him on his cell phone, and it sounded like he was talking to the police. We then made some small talk and in the course of that conversation, I asked him how he got in touch with the police so fast. He just told me he dialed 911 and got them quickly. He then spotted an EMS truck pulling up, and said something about his leg bothering him a little, and went directly over to it. I agreed it might not be a bad idea to get it checked out.

After he went to the EMS truck, the tow-truck driver, who had recently pulled up, came over to me to talk. He asked me if I knew the driver of the other vehicle. I said, "No, why should I?"

"He's a cop."

"Really? And how do you know that?"

"Hey, I've been around for a while. Trust me. I know him well. Watch him."

It was at that point things began to make sense. That pretty much answered the question as to how he reached the police so quickly. The police who were at the scene of the accident told me I had nothing to worry about, and there would be no citations given to either driver. It appeared neither driver was at fault. I slowly began to understand how things were going so smoothly. It was only much later on that I received notification the officer was suing my company and me.

I had already notified our corporate office of all the details of the accident, and they assured me I had absolutely nothing to worry about, whether or not I was at fault. Like all major corporations, they had a legal department that handled this sort of thing regularly. The other party would undoubtedly sue the company and they were always prepared for that.

Well, it was obvious the company knew what they were doing, and they were indeed ready for any eventuality. My wife has always been the worrier of the family, and this was no exception. She was afraid the police officer would sue us for everything we had, and I was trying to assure her it would not make much difference anyway, because we did not have all that much for him to get. She did not see my attempt at humor at all.

The version of the accident, as depicted by the police officer's lawyers, was quite amazing. I had to have been the worst driver in the state of New York to be guilty of all the things of which I was being accused. They had completely turned everything around backwards to suit their needs. The cop's lawyers then sent me a scenario of the case the way they understood it, which would have indicated my guilt to all that they described, and that was a total fabrication of the truth.

When I was asked to appear in New York to give my own deposition, I merely told our corporate lawyer, who was defending me, that all I was prepared to do was tell the truth, which was 180 degrees off from the story that the officer's lawyer had. In two days, the lawyer called me back and told me not to come to New York. The case had ended. Apparently, there was an out of court settlement, and I never heard anything more. I always tell Deb not to worry. She seldom listens. It's all part of the big plan. That's exactly what makes life so great. Why on earth would I ever want a "yes" woman in my life? It would take all the challenges out of it. I would have nothing left for which to strive, and, of course, if I were ever to reach for and attain such a goal, I would not have a clue as to what to do with it.

Conclusion

I have classified this book as a memoir, and most of us know memoirs normally reflect autobiographical elements. It is also my humble opinion, if one is to write an autobiography, he or she should be a prominent figure in one way or another. Who the heck do I think I am to write an autobiography? Very few of you who have read this book have a clue who I am, other than what you have read about me, or perhaps read in my previous book, MILITARY LIFE SERVICE OR CAREER - A SOLDIER'S PERSPECTIVE. I am no celebrity or anyone who has ever made newspaper headlines. I am no better, important or well known than most of you, and perhaps less so. I had a significant message to share with as many as I could reach, who might benefit in some way from it, and, yes, it is about me; therefore, I call it a memoir. One of those benefits, I would hope, might be just to get a good chuckle or two.

I hope I have shown I have had an extremely rewarding life so far, but not one that has not had its share of challenges, disappointments and failures. I think the beauty of the whole message is that my story is anything but unique. I hope you have enjoyed the humorous aspects of some of the very strange things that have happened to me, and benefitted from some that were more serious. There are probably millions of people, who have experienced much of what I have. I hope those of you who have already lived a good deal of life can identify with a great deal of it, and, if you are still quite young, you will be able to look forward to such things, the good along with the seemingly bad.

I mention the "seemingly bad" only because what really does seem to be bad at the time it happens very frequently turns out to be for the good. I can only speak for myself, but for me all things that have ever happened in my life have turned out to be for the ultimate good. That is why we must trust in our God to do, or allow to happen what is best for us. It is so easy to look up and say, "Lord, what kind of a god are You to allow such things to happen?" Worse yet, many ask, "What kind of a god would do such things?" The answer can be quite simple: a loving God.

I hope I made clear the idea that life is full of challenges, disappointments and even failures in order to motivate us to do better and try harder to find that ultimate success. To phrase it somewhat differently, I made it to beyond seventy years old, but not without a few hairpin curves along the way. I fully intend, God willing, to make it another forty years or so before my own end times. I mentioned I now feel success right now, but that by no means should indicate I am all through looking for additional successes for my future. Hey, maybe I could use a few more failures to go along with them. I hope not, but one never knows, right?

Conclusion | 281

In many ways, I feel I have hardly gotten started. You are now reading this book, and I can presume I have been successful in having published a book that will help or entertain some of my readers. By itself, this is great, and I still have a humor book coming up right behind this one, and I have other writing projects in the works. I have so many ideas floating around in my head I am not sure I have time in this life to finish all of them. That is exactly the way we should all be looking at life. Do you know your purpose in life? We all have at least one, but most of us don't have a clue what it might be. We may die and still not know. Even though I may have already found mine, I don't know for sure. It may still be out there waiting for my discovery.

Many feel they have missed something extremely important in life if they have not figured out their purpose. I am not at all convinced we should ever have to know our purpose. Our Creator knows, and that is probably all that is important. Maybe we are not supposed to know until we meet Him, when we are finished with it. I am looking forward to the time when my Creator and I can rejoice together over my having accomplished His goal for me. I am presuming that He will see to it that I do it. Why should we ever presume anything else? He is the One Who is in control. I am certainly not. I think it would be dangerous to think any other way.

Even if you were to think you are the "master of your fate and the captain of your soul," you should still have the same attitude toward your life, in that you will always strive to be successful in all of your endeavors, based, if nothing else, upon your faith in yourself. You have an obligation to develop an undying confidence in yourself and know you will face obstacles along the path of life. If you conquer all of those obstacles and totally ignore all of the little failures in life, you will undoubtedly be successful in the end. Strive until the day you die to achieve more successes. You will die with a smile. That's my plan. Is it a great plan or what? I recommend it to all.

Make your life a great one.

Take a few risks if that seems to be the way.

About the Author

John McClarren is a retired US Army infantry officer, having served for over thirty years before his retirement as a lieutenant colonel. During his Army active duty career, after a year as an enlisted man, he was a training officer at Fort Polk Louisiana, an infantry platoon leader in the Republic of Vietnam, a plans and operations officer at Sixth Army Headquarters at the Presidio of San Francisco, and finally both a psychological operations officer and an infantry company commander with the Second Infantry Division in the Republic of Korea. After coming off of active duty he remained in the reserve components of the Army until his retirement.

Besides his military service, John graduated from the University of Arizona with a BA in secondary education, majoring in German and minoring in English. He did graduate work at the University of Arizona as well as the University of San Diego in the fields of German, secondary education and counselor education. He taught high school German and English at Torrey Pines High School, Del Mar, California for twenty years. As well as teaching, he was active in the local teachers' union as site representative for many years, and served as Grievance

Chairperson for the district. That ended his full-time teaching career, whereupon he moved his family to northern Michigan where he still lives today.

With the tremendous length and diversity of his military career, his educational background with a teaching career, and his phenomenal array of travels around most of the world, John McClarren could not be better suited for writing TAKING RISKS DEFINING LIFE - A SOLDIER'S MEMOIR, as well as his previous book, MILITARY LIFE SERVICE OR CAREER - A SOLDIER'S PERSPECTIVE. They have both been naturals for him.

Abbreviations

AIT – advanced individual training

BCT – basic combat training

CIB – combat infantry badge

EIB – expert infantry badge

LIB – light infantry brigade

MOS – military occupational specialty

NCO – non-commissioned officer

NVA – North Vietnamese Army

OCS – officer candidate school

PF – popular forces

PTSD – post traumatic stress disorder

ROTC – reserve officers training corps

RPG – rocket propelled grenade

RTO – radio telephone operator

VC – Viet Cong

THANK YOU

There are several people on my list of those to whom to give thanks. Again, as in my first book, the most important has to be my wife, Debbie, for, first of all, just enduring some of my personal risk-taking. She was the one who took the brunt of much of it. She was also the first person I always interrupted from her unbelievably busy life to listen to my ramblings from portions of my manuscript.

I thank my good friend and editor, Philip Espinosa, for his expertise in formatting and editing the manuscript, inserting photographs and generally putting together everything, including the front and back covers of the book to make it readable and appealing to the eye in order to catch the attention of potential readers. He is a resource without whom I could not publish with such confidence.

Lastly, I want to thank all of the named and unnamed characters I reference as examples within the pages of this book. Without them there would be no merit or substance whatsoever. They have all contributed to influencing my life in a very positive way.

Preview of Military Life Service or Career – A Soldier's Perspective

John McClarren shares an honest look at what military life is all about. This book is for those thinking about military as a service or a career. You will experience humor, terror, suspense and adventure. Leadership, maturity and personal growth are also a natural result of the military experience.

From the Introduction:

In the pitch-black darkness of an open rice paddy a streak of lightening awakens us from a mesmerized state, followed by a clap of thunder, rattling us to the core. We are then drenched by torrential rain, all of those things expected during the summer monsoons of Southeast Asia. We have set up our night position, complete with razor-sharp concertina wire surrounding our company perimeter, unusual for us, unless trouble is anticipated.

We have been in heavy contact with North Vietnamese Army (NVA) regulars most of the day, and there is no doubt in anyone's mind that our enemy is still nearby tonight. The night rolls on, and the rain is not letting up. We are laying in rice paddies with water up to our shoulders, plagued with that physical stress, and at the same time the mental stress of an anticipated, impending attack. Just as suddenly as the first clap of thunder broke the stillness of the night, automatic weapons fire suddenly interrupts the monotony of the falling rain. Along with those bursts of gunfire are the resounding rocket-propelled grenade (RPG) explosions, as well as those from our own grenade launchers and hand grenades, lighting up the sky and the surrounding area just enough to spot, momentarily, a phenomenal number of NVA regulars charging our perimeter.

Our bodies tingle, our muscles flex and our reflex reactions sharpen to a hair trigger. There are NVA everywhere! Never have we seen so many of them all at one time. We open up with everything we've got, whether or not we can see our targets. Every shot counts, as this is no time to run short on ammunition. The enemy charging us, and the dead hanging in the wire, give an eerie feeling, which increases as they continue to come through the wire.

As this insane fire fight persists, now with our own artillery rounds landing closer and closer, adding to its effectiveness and to the chaos, an RPG round whizzes by my head and sticks in the mud dyke against which I am lying, hardly three feet away from my head! The man closest to me is my platoon sergeant, Sergeant Joe Terrell, and that round is right between us! This is the most terrifying experience probably in either of our lives, not just because this has been a close call; we have already had plenty of those. It is, rather, because it is looking death right in the face, as the two of us are watching that round, waiting for a delayed detonation to end our lives right here and now.

From Chapter One:

For the armed forces of the United States to maintain superiority throughout the world, a few things are absolutely necessary to maintain a continuing state of readiness. We need to maintain our troop strength, our equipment levels in regard to quality and quantity, and the focus and frequency of training in all branches of the military, and at all levels of command. Indeed, that training can never end, and our country can never weaken its resolve in those efforts, or we will find ourselves diminishing in our effectiveness, only to become a second-rate military force. We cannot afford that. Training for the individual begins the first day the recruit reports for duty. He or she begins basic training, or boot camp, and that is only the beginning phase of a series of training levels through which that man or woman will go. Then, of course, beyond the individual, there is unit training at every level of command, from the squad-, section- or team-sized unit right up to the Commander-in Chief, the President.

Most Americans have heard the horror stories of boot camps from all branches of the military service. There are likely as many versions of the boot camp experience in each branch of the military service as there are people who have experienced it first-hand. Most of the colorful stories that abound probably come from the Marines who have always been notorious for having the toughest of all programs. It is probably still true, but none of these programs is designed to be the proverbial "piece of cake." Most people who have graduated from such training probably perceived it at the time as one of the most difficult experiences of their lives. That feeling, however, generally subsides shortly thereafter and becomes just another invaluable experience that contributes to the overall development of the individual as a Marine, soldier, sailor or airman.

My perspective is that of an old soldier. I was Army most of my life, though I was born and raised in a Navy town, and later thrived among Marines; in this case, "survived" might be a more appropriate term. My experiences with boot camp or basic training were not as traumatic as some might have you believe their experiences were. I started with a distinct advantage, however. I had prior military experience before enlisting in the Army, which included one year of Air Force sponsored Civil Air Patrol in my first year of high school, Army junior ROTC (Reserve Officers Training Corps) in my next two years of high school and a couple of years of Air Force ROTC in college. That put me "miles" ahead of most of my peers, or seemingly so, when in actuality all it did was get me into a good deal more trouble than I would have had without it. The very first thing my drill sergeant did was make me the platoon leader of my basic training platoon.

That certainly brings up an old memory, that of Drill Sergeant Moyer. That man's face is embedded so deeply in my memory banks that I'll take his image to the grave. Some have deeply seated hatred for their old basic training drill sergeants, but that would by no means constitute my feelings for Drill Sergeant Moyer. I have nothing but the utmost respect for that man. I have no clue, of course, whether he is alive or dead today, but, as most of us know, "Old soldiers never die; they just fade away." He has to be one of those. I use this example, because so many who have gone through this experience will be able to identify with it, and my younger readers may well have similar experiences in the future. At the very least, they will be memories forever.

Made in the USA
Middletown, DE
09 September 2015